Make Sh** Happen

Sharpen Your Intuition

Deborah LeBlanc, CCHt, CACHA

Copyright © 2024 Deborah LeBlanc, CCHt, CACHA

All rights reserved.

The contents of this book may not be reproduced, duplicated, or transmitted without direct written permission from the author.

Under no circumstances will any legal responsibility or blame be held against the publisher for any reparation, damages, or monetary loss due to the information herein, either directly or indirectly.

Legal Notice

This book is copyright-protected. This is only for personal use. You cannot amend, distribute, sell, use, quote, or paraphrase any part of the content within this book without the consent of the author.

Disclaimer Notice

Please note the information contained within this document is for educational and entertainment purposes only. Every attempt has been made to provide accurate, up-to-date, reliable, and complete information. No warranties of any kind are expressed or implied. Readers acknowledge that the author is not engaging in the rendering of legal, financial, medical, or professional advice. The content of this book has been derived from various sources. Please consult a licensed professional before attempting any techniques outlined in this book.

By reading this document, the reader agrees that under no circumstances is the author responsible for any losses, direct or indirect, which are incurred as a result of the use of the information contained within this document, including, but not limited to, errors, omissions, or inaccuracies.

Table of Contents

Introduction	7
Chapter 1: Get Your Mind Right	10
Why Should You Meditate?	11
How to Meditate?	13
Technology "Fast" or "Cleanse"	21
Spend Time outside and Engage in Enjoyable Activities	25
Conclusion	26
Chapter 2: Test Yourself	28
Types of Intuition Scale	29
The Rational Experiential Inventory	35
Myers-Briggs Type Indicator	38
Reflect on Past Experiences	41
Conclusion	42
Chapter 3: Dissect Your Dreams	44
Introduction to the Science of Dreams	45
Benefits of Journaling Dreams	48
Exploring Dream Questions	53
Conclusion	56

Chapter 4: Be Conscious of the Subconscious	58
The Nature of Intuition	59
The Dual Process Theory	63
The Power of Intuition	65
Overcome Intuitive Biases	69
Further Reading or Resources	72
Conclusion	73
Chapter 5: Work with Your Intuition	75
You Can Develop Intuition	76
Work with Direct Intuition	77
Work with Indirect Intuition	80
Integrate Intuition into Decision-Making	82
Overcome Challenges and Skepticism	83
Conclusion	85
Chapter 6: Eliminate Bad Habits	87
Impact of Bad Habits on Intuition	88
The Psychology of Cognitive Biases	90
Choose Environments Conducive to Intuition	92
Breaking the Multitasking Trap	93
Prioritize Mental Health for Enhanced Intuition	96
Develop Positive Habits	97
Conclusion	98
Chapter 7: Practice and Improve	100
The Power of Social Cues	101
Practice Intuition through Structured Routines	102
Overcome the Fear of Imperfection	106
Cultivating Intuition through Feedback	108
Leveraging Technology and Resources	109
Track Progress and Celebrate Successes	112
Conclusion	114

Chapter 8: Get Your Sh** Together	115
How to Navigate Challenges and Setbacks?	116
Prioritize Mental Health	117
Be Mindful and Meditate	119
Just Relax	121
Seek Support for Mental Health	122
Celebrate Progress and Growth	124
Conclusion	126
Conclusion	128
Bibliography	130

Introduction

Intuition, often hailed as the silent force guiding our decisions, is a fascinating aspect of human cognition that transcends the boundaries of conscious reasoning. Intuition can be understood as the innate ability to comprehend or sense something without the need for explicit analysis or logical deduction. It operates swiftly and effortlessly, providing us with insights and understandings that may elude conscious awareness.

The significance of intuition in human cognition cannot be overstated. It serves as a fundamental aspect of decision-making, allowing individuals to navigate complex situations and make choices swiftly, often under conditions of uncertainty. Whether it's a gut feeling urging us to trust or doubt or a sudden burst of inspiration illuminating a creative endeavor, intuition plays a pivotal role in shaping our actions and responses.

One of the defining characteristics of intuition is its elusive nature. Unlike rational thought processes, which can be dissected and analyzed, intuition often operates on a subconscious level, beyond the reach of conscious awareness. It manifests as a subtle whisper, a fleeting sensation, or an inexplicable knowing, making it challenging to pin down and define with precision.

However, despite its enigmatic nature, intuition has been a subject of fascination and inquiry across various disciplines. Philosophers, psychologists, and neuroscientists alike have grappled with the question of what intuition is and how it operates within the human mind. Some propose that intuition is a form of implicit learning, drawing upon past experiences and knowledge stored in memory. Others suggest that it arises from the integration of disparate pieces of information, synthesized into a coherent understanding without conscious effort.

Indeed, there is no singular definition of intuition, as it encompasses a broad spectrum of experiences and phenomena. Yet despite its elusive nature, intuition remains a potent force in human cognition, guiding us through the complexities of everyday life and offering insights that transcend the limitations of conscious thought.

In essence, intuition is a testament to the remarkable capabilities of the human mind, offering a glimpse into the vast reservoir of knowledge and wisdom that lies beyond the realm of conscious awareness. By embracing and honing our intuitive abilities, we can tap into a wellspring of insight and understanding, enriching our lives and enhancing our capacity for decision-making and creativity.

However, before we dive into the nitty-gritty of intuition, let's address the elephant in the room: What's holding you back from reaching your intuitive potential? We'll touch on this briefly here, but fear not, we'll tackle it head-on as we progress through the chapters.

So, what's next? We'll kick things off by getting your mind right. From meditation to taking a break from technology to simply spending time outdoors, we'll explore simple yet effective ways to clear the mental clutter and pave the way for intuitive insights.

But this isn't just a passive journey. You'll be put to the test. We'll introduce various tests and scales to help you understand your intuitive strengths and weaknesses. Remember, though, nothing beats your own personal insights, so we'll encourage you to reflect on past instances where your intuition served you well.

Then, we'll dive into the fascinating world of dreams and the role they play in intuition. Journaling your dreams can uncover hidden emotions and insights, guiding you toward a deeper understanding of yourself.

Next up, we'll delve into the subconscious mind. It's where intuition thrives, constantly processing information beneath the surface of our awareness. We'll explore the distinction between automatic intuition and deliberate thought processes, shedding light on how to harness both for maximum effectiveness.

But enough theory, it's time to get practical. We'll discuss how to actively work with your intuition, from recognizing direct signals to decoding indirect cues. It's all about practice and refinement, honing your intuition like a fine-tuned instrument.

Of course, no journey is without its obstacles. We'll tackle bad habits head-on, addressing the cognitive biases and distractions that can derail your intuitive progress. It's about creating an environment conducive to growth and learning, while also taking care of your mental health along the way.

And as we wrap up, we'll leave you with a dose of motivation and encouragement. This isn't just about improving your memory; it's about taking control of your life and making things happen.

Now, are you ready to tap into your intuition and unlock your full potential? Then make sh** happen and improve your intuition.

Chapter One

Get Your Mind Right

In a world where the constant barrage of stimuli threatens to overwhelm us, finding moments of clarity and peace can seem like an impossible task. But amid the chaos, a simple yet profound practice holds the key to reclaiming our inner calm and intuition: meditation.

In the first part of this chapter, we'll dive into the transformative power of meditation. We'll explore practical steps to incorporate meditation into your daily routine, demystifying the process and highlighting its profound benefits. From mindfulness to loving-kindness, we'll uncover a variety of techniques designed to quiet the mind and cultivate a deeper connection with yourself.

But meditation is just the beginning. In the second part of this chapter, we'll tackle the pervasive influence of technology on our mental well-being and intuition. We'll discuss the importance of taking breaks from screens and digital devices and explore strategies for implementing a technology "fast" or "cleanse" to recalibrate our focus and clarity.

Finally, we'll turn our attention to the rejuvenating power of nature and enjoyable activities. In the third part of this chapter, we'll delve into the restorative benefits of spending time outside and engaging in activities that bring you joy. Whether it's a leisurely hike in the woods or immersing yourself in a creative pursuit, we'll uncover how these experiences nourish the mind, body, and spirit and foster a deeper connection with the world around you.

So, if you're ready to get your mind right and reclaim your inner peace and intuition, enjoy this journey of self-discovery and transformation. Explore the myriad ways in which meditation, technology fast, and joyful experiences can help you navigate the challenges of modern life with clarity, purpose, and presence.

Why Should You Meditate?

Meditation, often perceived as a mystical practice reserved for yogis and spiritual gurus, is actually a simple yet profoundly transformative tool accessible to anyone seeking to enhance their intuition and overall well-being. In the hustle and bustle of modern life, where distractions abound and stress levels soar, carving out a few moments each day to quiet the mind through meditation can be the key to unlocking a deeper connection with oneself and the world around us.

At its core, meditation is about cultivating a sense of inner peace and awareness. It offers a sanctuary amid the chaos, providing a refuge where one can retreat from the noise of daily life and find solace in the stillness within. In today's fast-paced society, where our attention is constantly pulled in a million different directions, this ability to quiet the mind and center ourselves becomes increasingly invaluable.

One of the most significant benefits of meditation is its ability to sharpen intuition. Intuition, often described as a gut feeling or inner knowing, is our innate ability to understand something instinctively, without the need for conscious reasoning. Through regular meditation practice, we can cultivate a heightened sense of awareness that allows us to tap into this intuitive wisdom more readily. By quieting the incessant chatter of the mind, we create space for intuitive insights to emerge, guiding us toward decisions that align with our deepest truths and desires.

But the benefits of meditation extend far beyond just intuition. Research has shown that regular meditation practice can lead to improvements in mental clarity, focus, and cognitive function. By training the mind to stay present and focused on the present moment, meditation helps to sharpen our mental faculties, enabling us to think more clearly and make better decisions in all aspects of life.

Moreover, meditation is a powerful tool for stress reduction. In today's high-pressure world, stress has become an epidemic, wreaking havoc on our physical, mental, and emotional well-being. Fortunately, meditation offers a natural antidote to the stress response, triggering the relaxation response and promoting a state of deep relaxation and calm. By cultivating a regular meditation practice, we can learn to manage stress more effectively, leading to greater resilience and inner peace.

Perhaps most importantly, meditation serves as a gateway to connecting with our inner selves and intuition. In the silence of meditation, we have the opportunity to turn inward and explore the depths of our own consciousness. Here, we can uncover hidden truths, unravel subconscious patterns, and gain insights into our deepest desires and motivations. Through this process of self-discovery, we forge a deeper connection with ourselves and cultivate a greater sense of inner harmony and alignment.

Meditation is a powerful practice with profound implications for our mental, emotional, and spiritual well-being. By quieting the mind, sharpening intuition, and fostering a deeper connection with ourselves, meditation empowers us to navigate life's challenges with greater clarity, confidence, and grace. So, whether you're a seasoned meditator or a curious beginner, I invite you to explore the transformative power of meditation and discover the profound benefits it has to offer.

How to Meditate?

Embarking on a journey of meditation may seem daunting at first, but fear not, for it is a journey well worth undertaking. Meditation is not reserved for the enlightened few; it is a practice that anyone can cultivate with dedication and patience. In this section, we will explore some basic meditation techniques, provide step-by-step instructions for beginners, and underscore the importance of consistency and practice in reaping the rich rewards that meditation has to offer.

Types of Meditation

1. **Mindfulness Meditation**

Mindfulness meditation is often considered the cornerstone of meditation practices, drawing from ancient Buddhist teachings and adapted into secular contexts. At its core, mindfulness meditation involves bringing focused attention to the present moment with openness, curiosity, and nonjudgment. Practitioners typically begin by anchoring their awareness to the breath, sensations in the body, or sounds in the environment. As thoughts, emotions, and external distractions arise, practitioners are encouraged to observe them without attachment or reaction, allowing them to come and go like clouds passing through the sky. Through consistent practice, mindfulness meditation cultivates greater self-awareness, emotional resilience, and a deep sense of inner peace.

2. Transcendental Meditation (TM)

TM is a technique rooted in ancient Vedic traditions and popularized by Maharishi Mahesh Yogi in the 1950s. During TM, practitioners sit comfortably with closed eyes and silently repeat a specific mantra given to them by a trained instructor. The mantra serves as a focal point for the mind, allowing it to naturally settle into a state of deep relaxation and transcendent awareness. Unlike mindfulness meditation, which involves observing experiences as they arise, TM aims to effortlessly transcend ordinary thought processes and access a silent, pure awareness beyond the surface level of consciousness. Research has shown that regular practice of TM can reduce stress, improve cognitive function, and promote overall well-being.

3. Loving-Kindness Meditation (Metta)

Loving-kindness meditation, also known as Metta meditation, is a practice rooted in Buddhist traditions that involves intentionally cultivating feelings of love, compassion, and goodwill toward oneself and others. Practitioners typically begin by generating feelings of loving-kindness toward themselves, silently reciting phrases such as "May I be happy, may I be healthy, may I be safe, may I live with ease." They then extend these wishes outward, first to loved ones, then to acquaintances, and eventually to all beings without exception. Metta meditation not only fosters a sense of connection and empathy but also helps to dissolve feelings of resentment, hostility, and isolation. According to Galante et al., research, published in the *Journal of Consulting and Clinical Psychology* in 2014, suggests that regular practice of Metta meditation can enhance positive emotions, reduce symptoms of depression and anxiety, and strengthen social bonds.

4. Guided Visualization

Guided visualization is a form of meditation that utilizes imagery and visualization techniques to evoke specific mental images, sensations, or experiences. Practitioners typically listen to recorded audio or receive guidance from a teacher who leads them through a series of verbal instructions. These instructions may involve imagining oneself in a peaceful natural setting, visualizing a desired outcome or goal, or engaging in symbolic imagery for healing and transformation. By engaging the mind's creative faculties, guided visualization can help reduce stress, enhance relaxation, and increase self-confidence and motivation. It is often used in conjunction with other therapeutic modalities such as hypnotherapy, cognitive behavioral therapy, and mindfulness-based stress reduction.

5. Mantra Meditation

Mantra meditation is a practice that involves silently repeating a sacred sound, word, or phrase (mantra) to focus the mind and induce a meditative state. Mantras can be traditional Sanskrit phrases, such as "Om Mani Padme Hum" or "So Hum," or personal affirmations chosen for their significance and resonance. The repetition of the mantra serves to quiet the chatter of the mind and cultivate a sense of inner peace and clarity. Unlike mindfulness meditation, which emphasizes present-moment awareness, mantra meditation provides a single point of focus that can help practitioners transcend ordinary consciousness and access deeper states of awareness. Mantra meditation is commonly practiced in Hindu, Buddhist, and Sikh traditions, as well as in contemporary spiritual practices and self-help modalities.

6. Body Scan Meditation

Body scan meditation is a mindfulness practice that involves systematically directing attention to different parts of the body, starting from the top of the head and moving down to the toes. As practitioners scan through each body part, they observe any sensations, tension, or discomfort present without judgment or resistance. By bringing gentle awareness to the body, practitioners can release physical tension, reduce stress, and cultivate a deeper connection between mind and body. Body scan meditation is often used as a relaxation technique, a tool for managing chronic pain or illness, and a way to develop greater body awareness and acceptance. Furthermore, research, by Black et al. published in 2015, shows that regular practice of body scan meditation can improve sleep quality, reduce symptoms of anxiety and depression, and enhance overall well-being.

7. **Breath Awareness Meditation**

Breath awareness meditation is a foundational practice that involves focusing attention on the breath as it moves in and out of the body. Practitioners may observe the natural rhythm, depth, and quality of their breath without trying to control or manipulate it. By anchoring awareness to the breath, practitioners can cultivate mindfulness, calm the fluctuations of the mind, and deepen their capacity for presence and relaxation. Breath awareness meditation is often used as a starting point for beginners and can be practiced in various postures, such as sitting, lying down, or walking. As practitioners develop greater sensitivity to their breath, they may also discover insights into the interconnectedness of body, mind, and spirit.

8. **Zen Meditation (Zazen)**

Zen meditation, also known as Zazen, is a central practice in Zen Buddhism that involves sitting in a specific posture (typically cross-legged on a cushion or bench) and maintaining focused awareness on the breath, body, or a koan (a paradoxical question or statement). Unlike other forms of meditation that emphasize relaxation or visualization, Zazen emphasizes disciplined attention and direct insight into the nature of reality. Practitioners may sit in silence for extended periods, facing a wall or in a group setting under the guidance of a teacher (*roshi*). Through the sustained practice of Zazen, practitioners aim to develop greater concentration, equanimity, and insight into the nature of mind and existence. Zazen is often considered a path to awakening or enlightenment in Zen Buddhism and is characterized by its simplicity, austerity, and emphasis on direct experience.

9. Chakra Meditation

Chakra meditation is a practice rooted in Hindu and yogic traditions that focuses on visualizing and balancing the body's energy centers, known as chakras. According to these traditions, there are seven main chakras located along the spine, each associated with specific qualities, colors, and psychological functions. During chakra meditation, practitioners may use visualization, breathwork, sound, or affirmations to cleanse, activate, and harmonize the chakras, promoting physical, emotional, and spiritual well-being. For example, practitioners may visualize a specific color or geometric shape associated with each chakra while directing breath and awareness to that area of the body. Chakra meditation is often used as a tool for healing, personal growth, and spiritual awakening, helping practitioners tap into their innate potential and connect with the subtle energies of the universe.

10. Movement-Based Meditation

Movement-based meditation encompasses a variety of practices that integrate gentle movement with mindfulness and awareness. Tai chi, qigong, and walking meditation are among the most well-known forms of movement-based meditation, each with its own unique principles and techniques. Tai chi and qigong originated in ancient China and involve slow, flowing movements coordinated with deep breathing and focused attention. These practices promote balance, flexibility, and vitality while cultivating inner calm and mental clarity. Walking meditation, on the other hand, involves walking slowly and deliberately with full awareness of each step and breath. Practitioners may focus on the sensations of the feet touching the ground, the movement of the body, or the sights and sounds of the surrounding environment. Movement-based meditation is particularly beneficial for those who find stillness challenging or prefer a more dynamic and embodied approach to meditation. It can be practiced indoors or outdoors, alone or in a group, and offers a pathway to mindfulness and well-being through the integration of body, mind, and spirit.

11. Self-inquiry

Meditation, when approached through self-inquiry, is a practice of actively exploring one's inner landscape. It involves turning attention inward to observe thoughts, emotions, and sensations without judgment. In self-inquiry meditation, practitioners ask themselves questions designed to uncover deeper truths about their experiences and beliefs. By maintaining a curious and non-reactive attitude, individuals can gain insights into their patterns of thinking and behavior. Self-inquiry meditation encourages a direct investigation into the nature of the self, leading to greater self-awareness and understanding. This technique is particularly effective for those seeking clarity and resolution in areas of their lives where they feel stuck or uncertain. Through consistent practice, individuals can cultivate a deeper connection with themselves and navigate life with greater clarity and authenticity.

By exploring the diverse range of meditation techniques available, individuals can find the practices that resonate most deeply with their needs, preferences, and spiritual aspirations. Whether seeking stress relief, emotional healing, or spiritual awakening, the journey of meditation offers endless opportunities for growth, self-discovery, and transformation.

Guided Meditation

For those who prefer a more guided approach, guided meditation can be an excellent starting point. Guided meditation involves following the instructions of a meditation teacher or recorded audio to lead you through the practice. There are countless guided meditations available online, covering a wide range of topics from stress relief to self-love to spiritual awakening.

One of the primary benefits of guided meditation is accessibility. For beginners, guided meditation provides a supportive entry point into the practice, offering clear instructions and encouragement to help overcome initial barriers such as restlessness or wandering thoughts. The guidance provided in a guided meditation session serves as an anchor, helping individuals stay focused and engaged throughout the practice.

Guided meditation sessions typically begin with relaxation techniques to calm the mind and body, such as deep breathing exercises or progressive muscle relaxation. As the session progresses, the instructor or recorded voice leads participants through a series of visualizations, affirmations, or mindfulness exercises designed to cultivate specific qualities or states of consciousness.

For example, a guided meditation may focus on promoting relaxation and stress relief by guiding participants to visualize a peaceful scene in nature, such as a tranquil forest or serene beach. The instructor may encourage participants to imagine the sights, sounds, and sensations of this environment, allowing them to immerse themselves fully in the experience and let go of tension and worry.

Guided meditations can also target specific areas of personal development, such as building self-confidence, fostering compassion, or overcoming negative thought patterns. Through guided imagery and affirmations, participants are guided to explore their inner landscape, identify limiting beliefs or emotional blocks, and cultivate positive qualities and attitudes.

Guided meditation also offers a sense of connection and support, particularly when practiced in a group setting or with a live instructor. Participants can benefit from the collective energy and shared intention of the group, enhancing their sense of belonging and motivation to continue their meditation practice.

Another advantage of guided meditation is its adaptability to different preferences and needs. With a wide range of guided meditation recordings available online and in various formats, individuals can choose sessions tailored to their specific goals, interests, and time constraints. Whether seeking relaxation, stress relief, personal growth, or spiritual exploration, there is a guided meditation available to suit virtually any preference or intention.

The Right Mindset for Meditation

Like any skill, meditation requires dedication and commitment to see results. It's not enough to meditate sporadically; to truly reap the benefits, you must make meditation a regular part of your daily routine. Set aside a specific time each day to meditate, whether it's first thing in the morning, during your lunch break, or before bed. Consistency is key—even just a few minutes of meditation each day can yield profound results over time.

As you embark on your meditation journey, remember to approach the practice with an open mind and a compassionate heart. Be patient with yourself and allow yourself to progress at your own pace. There will be days when meditation feels effortless and serene, and there will be days when it feels challenging and chaotic. Embrace each moment as it comes, knowing that every moment spent in meditation brings you one step closer to greater peace, clarity, and self-awareness.

The right mindset for meditation is one of openness, curiosity, and acceptance. It's about approaching the practice with a nonjudgmental attitude, allowing thoughts, emotions, and sensations to arise without trying to control or suppress them. Instead of striving for a particular outcome or experience, the ideal mindset involves simply being present in the moment and observing whatever arises with a sense of detachment.

Also, keep in mind that maintaining an attitude of kindness and compassion toward oneself is crucial. This includes being forgiving of perceived failures or lapses in focus during meditation sessions. Instead of berating oneself for getting lost in thought, it's more beneficial to gently guide the attention back to the present moment with a sense of kindness and understanding.

Technology "Fast" or "Cleanse"

Technology has undoubtedly revolutionized the way we live, work, and connect with others. From smartphones to social media to streaming services, technology has become an integral part of our daily lives. However, while technology has brought many benefits, its excessive use can also have detrimental effects on our mental well-being and intuition.

Recognize the Potential Drawbacks of Constant Connectivity

In today's digitally driven world, the drawbacks of constant connectivity loom large. While technology promises efficiency and connectivity, its incessant demands can exact a heavy toll on our mental well-being. The constant influx of notifications, emails, and social media updates serves as a relentless distraction, eroding our ability to focus and think deeply. This perpetual state of distraction not only impedes our productivity but also undermines our capacity to tap into our intuition and make thoughtful decisions.

Moreover, the omnipresence of technology blurs the boundaries between work and personal life, leaving us feeling constantly tethered to our devices. This lack of separation can lead to heightened stress levels, exhaustion, and burnout. The pressure to constantly stay connected and available further exacerbates these issues, leaving little room for relaxation or rejuvenation.

Recognizing these drawbacks is crucial for safeguarding our mental health and reclaiming control over our digital lives. By acknowledging the negative impact of constant connectivity, we can begin to set boundaries, prioritize self-care, and carve out moments of digital detoxification. Only by confronting the detrimental effects of technology head-on can we hope to cultivate a healthier relationship with it and restore balance to our lives.

Explore the Concept of a Technology Cleanse

Exploring the concept of a technology cleanse unveils a powerful strategy for restoring mental clarity and reclaiming control over our digital lives. In essence, a technology cleanse involves intentionally disconnecting from digital devices and platforms to reduce distractions and cultivate mindfulness. By stepping away from the constant stream of notifications and information overload, we create space to reconnect with ourselves, our thoughts, and our intuition.

During a technology cleanse, we prioritize activities that nourish our minds and bodies, such as spending time outdoors, engaging in creative pursuits, or simply enjoying moments of quiet reflection. This intentional break from technology allows us to recharge our mental batteries, reduce stress levels, and gain perspective on our relationship with digital technology.

Moreover, a technology cleanse offers an opportunity to reassess our priorities and habits, enabling us to make more conscious choices about how we engage with technology in the future. By setting aside dedicated periods for digital detoxification, we establish healthier boundaries around our technology use and cultivate a greater sense of balance in our lives.

Ultimately, exploring the concept of a technology cleanse empowers us to take back control over our attention and mental energy, fostering greater clarity, presence, and well-being in the process.

Strategies for Implementing a Technology Cleanse Effectively

Implementing a technology cleanse effectively involves thoughtful planning and intentional action to ensure a successful disconnection from digital distractions. First, setting clear goals and boundaries is essential. Determine the duration and scope of your cleanse, whether it's a day-long break from screens or a week-long retreat from technology altogether. Establishing specific guidelines will help you stay focused and committed to your cleanse.

Next, communicate your intentions with others to garner support and accountability. Inform friends, family, and colleagues about your technology cleanse, and kindly ask for their understanding and cooperation during this time. Having a support system in place can make it easier to stick to your cleanse and resist the temptation to revert to old habits.

You also have to prepare alternative activities to fill the void left by digital distractions. Explore hobbies, spend time outdoors, or engage in mindfulness practices to occupy your time and soothe any discomfort that arises from disconnecting from technology.

Finally, be gentle with yourself and allow for flexibility in your approach. It's normal to experience withdrawal symptoms or moments of temptation during a technology cleanse. Instead of viewing these challenges as failures, see them as opportunities for growth and learning. Stay committed to your goals, but also be willing to adapt your strategy as needed to ensure a positive and fulfilling cleanse experience.

Finding the Right Balance

Finding balance between technology and intuition is crucial for effectively pursuing our goals in today's digital age. While technology offers valuable tools for productivity and efficiency, relying solely on digital solutions can often lead to a disconnect from our innate wisdom and intuition.

To strike this balance, it's essential to first cultivate awareness of how technology influences our decision-making processes. Recognize when technology serves as a helpful aid and when it becomes a barrier to accessing our intuition. By developing this awareness, we can intentionally integrate technology into our lives in a way that enhances rather than detracts from our intuitive abilities.

It is also important to prioritize practices that strengthen your intuition, such as mindfulness meditation, journaling, or spending time in nature. These activities provide opportunities to quiet the noise of technology and tune into our inner guidance system.

Additionally, establish rituals and boundaries around technology use to create space for intuition to thrive. Designate specific times for digital detoxification, limit screen time before bed, and prioritize face-to-face interactions over virtual communication whenever possible.

Ultimately, finding balance between technology and intuition requires ongoing mindfulness and intentionality. By honoring the unique strengths of both technology and our intuitive wisdom, we can harness their combined power to navigate life's challenges with clarity, purpose, and effectiveness.

Spend Time Outside and Engage in Enjoyable Activities

It's easy to become ensnared in the endless cycle of work, responsibilities, and digital distractions. However, amid the chaos lies a simple yet potent antidote for rejuvenating the mind and nourishing the soul: spending time outside and engaging in enjoyable activities.

Nature has a remarkable ability to soothe the spirit and restore balance to the mind. In today's increasingly urbanized world, many of us have become disconnected from the natural world, spending the majority of our time indoors surrounded by concrete walls and artificial light. Yet research published by the American Psychological Association has shown that spending time in nature can have profound effects on our mental and emotional well-being. Simply being in nature, whether it's taking a leisurely stroll through a park, hiking in the mountains, or lounging by the sea, can reduce stress levels, lower blood pressure, and improve mood. The sights, sounds, and smells of the natural world awaken our senses and remind us of our interconnectedness with all living things.

Moreover, engaging in enjoyable activities is essential for cultivating a sense of joy and fulfillment in life. Too often, we get caught up in the relentless pursuit of productivity and success, neglecting the simple pleasures that bring us true happiness. Engaging in activities that ignite our passions and spark our creativity, such as painting, gardening, playing music, or practicing yoga, is vital for our overall well-being. These activities provide an outlet for self-expression, allowing us to tap into our innate talents and strengths. They also offer a much-needed respite from the demands of daily life, giving us a chance to recharge our batteries and reconnect with the things that bring us joy.

But perhaps most importantly, spending time outside and engaging in enjoyable activities can enhance intuition by promoting creativity and mental relaxation. When we immerse ourselves in nature or lose ourselves in a favorite hobby, our minds enter a state of flow where time seems to stand still, and our thoughts flow freely. In this state of relaxed alertness, our intuition heightens, and we become more attuned to the subtle whispers of our inner wisdom. Ideas flow effortlessly, solutions to problems present themselves seemingly out of nowhere, and we gain clarity and insight into our deepest desires and aspirations.

In conclusion, spending time outside and engaging in enjoyable activities is essential for nourishing the mind, body, and soul. Whether it's basking in the beauty of nature or losing yourself in a favorite pastime, these experiences offer a sanctuary from the stresses of daily life and a pathway to greater creativity, joy, and intuition.

Conclusion

It's evident that the journey toward sharpening intuition and nurturing mental well-being is multifaceted and deeply personal. Through the exploration of meditation, we've discovered a powerful tool for quieting the mind, enhancing focus, and connecting with our inner wisdom. By embracing basic meditation techniques and committing to regular practice, we can cultivate a profound sense of inner peace and clarity that serves as the foundation for intuitive living.

Additionally, we've explored the impact of technology on our mental well-being and intuition, recognizing the importance of taking breaks from screens and digital devices to recalibrate our mental focus and clarity. By implementing strategies for a technology "fast" or "cleanse," we can create space for moments of silence and solitude, allowing our intuition to flourish amid the noise of modern life.

Furthermore, we've emphasized the rejuvenating power of spending time outside and engaging in enjoyable activities. Nature, with its inherent beauty and tranquility, provides a sanctuary for the soul, while enjoyable activities offer a pathway to greater creativity, joy, and intuition. By prioritizing time in nature and pursuing activities that bring us joy and fulfillment, we nourish our minds, bodies, and spirits, laying the groundwork for a life guided by intuition and purpose.

As we continue on this journey, let us remember to approach each moment with openness, curiosity, and compassion, trusting in the wisdom of our inner selves to guide us toward greater clarity, authenticity, and fulfillment. With dedication, practice, and a willingness to embrace the unknown, we can unlock the boundless potential that resides within each of us.

Chapter Two

Test Yourself

In this chapter, we dive into the world of intuition testing, exploring various assessments designed to shed light on our intuitive abilities. Tests, ranging from the Types of Intuition Scale to the Myers-Briggs Type Indicator, provide structured frameworks for understanding and categorizing intuition. They offer a structured approach to exploring our intuitive tendencies and can highlight patterns and preferences in our thinking styles.

However, it's essential to approach these tests with a critical eye. While they can provide valuable information, they do not capture the full complexity of intuition. Intuition is deeply personal and subjective, influenced by factors such as experience, emotion, and context. No test can fully capture the nuances of our intuitive abilities or predict how they will manifest in real-life situations.

Therefore, while tests can serve as useful starting points for self-reflection and exploration, they should not be viewed as definitive assessments of our intuitive capabilities. Personal insights, gained through reflection on past experiences and moments of intuitive clarity, are equally—if not more—valuable in understanding intuition.

Ultimately, the goal of exploring intuition through testing is not to achieve a certain score or label but rather to gain a deeper understanding of ourselves and how we perceive and process information intuitively. Tests can provide a framework for exploration and self-discovery, but they should be used in conjunction with personal reflection and real-life experiences.

You should approach these tests with curiosity, openness, and a willingness to learn. Use them as tools for exploration and growth while recognizing that our intuition is a rich and multifaceted aspect of our being that defies easy categorization. With this mindset, you can unlock new insights into your intuitive abilities and harness them to navigate life with greater clarity, confidence, and purpose.

Types of Intuition Scale

Introduction to the Types of Intuition Scale (TIS)

TIS, devised by Pretz and Totz in 2007, serves as a valuable tool for categorizing and understanding different facets of intuition: holistic, inferential, and affective. This scale aims to delineate various types of intuition, providing insights into how individuals perceive and process information intuitively. By categorizing intuition into distinct types, the TIS offers a structured framework for exploring and assessing intuitive abilities. It helps individuals gain clarity on their intuitive strengths and areas for growth, paving the way for deeper self-awareness and personal development.

Holistic Intuition

Holistic intuition is a profound and deeply intuitive understanding that transcends mere rational thought, encompassing a comprehensive awareness of the interconnectedness of all things. Unlike other forms of intuition that may focus on specific aspects or details, holistic intuition perceives the entirety of a situation, recognizing patterns, relationships, and underlying dynamics that may not be immediately apparent.

At its core, holistic intuition acknowledges that everything in the universe is interconnected and that each individual component plays a vital role in the larger whole. This intuitive understanding allows individuals to see beyond the surface level of reality, discerning the subtle interplay between various factors and influences.

Holistic intuition often arises from a sense of unity with the world around us, a deep connection to nature, and an awareness of the inherent harmony that exists in the universe. It is not bound by conventional logic or linear reasoning but instead operates on a higher level of consciousness, tapping into a universal wisdom that transcends individual experience.

Those who possess holistic intuition may find themselves drawn to practices such as meditation, mindfulness, and contemplation, as these activities help to quiet the mind and open the heart to the intuitive wisdom that lies within. Through these practices, individuals can cultivate a deeper sense of connection to themselves, to others, and to the world at large.

Holistic intuition is not limited to any particular domain or area of expertise; rather, it can be applied to all aspects of life, from personal relationships and career decisions to broader social and environmental issues. By tapping into this intuitive wisdom, individuals can make decisions that are aligned with their true values and purpose, leading to greater fulfillment and harmony in their lives.

In a world that often emphasizes rationality and logic above all else, holistic intuition serves as a powerful reminder of the importance of embracing our innate wisdom and connecting with the deeper truths that lie beyond the surface of reality. It invites us to trust in the intuitive guidance that arises from within and to recognize the interconnectedness of all things, fostering a sense of unity, compassion, and wholeness in our lives.

Inferential Intuition

Inferential intuition is a form of intuitive reasoning that allows individuals to draw insightful conclusions and make informed decisions based on limited information or incomplete data. Unlike purely rational or deductive reasoning, which relies on logical analysis and evidence, inferential intuition operates on a subconscious level, synthesizing subtle cues and patterns to arrive at intuitive insights.

At its essence, inferential intuition involves the subconscious processing of information, drawing upon past experiences, knowledge, and contextual clues to make intuitive judgments or predictions about future outcomes. This intuitive process often occurs rapidly and effortlessly, bypassing conscious thought and yielding insights that may not be immediately apparent through logical analysis alone.

One of the key features of inferential intuition is its ability to discern hidden connections or underlying patterns that may elude conscious awareness. By tapping into this intuitive faculty, individuals can uncover deeper meanings or insights that lie beneath the surface of apparent reality, shedding light on complex or ambiguous situations.

Inferential intuition often manifests in various forms, such as gut feelings, hunches, or instincts, which provide individuals with a sense of certainty or conviction about a particular course of action. While these intuitive impressions may be difficult to articulate or justify rationally, they are often based on a subconscious processing of relevant information and an intuitive understanding of the situation at hand.

Individuals who possess strong inferential intuition may find themselves able to anticipate future events, identify hidden opportunities, or navigate complex social dynamics with ease. This intuitive skill can be particularly valuable in decision-making contexts where time is limited and the stakes are high, allowing individuals to make quick, decisive choices based on their intuitive insights.

Developing inferential intuition requires practice, self-awareness, and a willingness to trust in one's intuitive faculties. By paying attention to subtle cues, listening to gut feelings, and reflecting on past experiences, individuals can hone their inferential intuition and become more adept at making intuitive judgments in various areas of their lives.

By tapping into this intuitive skill, individuals can uncover hidden connections, anticipate future outcomes, and navigate complex situations with confidence and clarity, ultimately leading to greater success and fulfillment in their lives.

Affective Intuition

Affective intuition, also known as emotional intuition, refers to the intuitive ability to perceive and understand emotions, both in oneself and in others. It involves the capacity to intuitively sense the emotional states of individuals, empathize with their feelings, and navigate interpersonal interactions with sensitivity and insight.

At its core, affective intuition operates through subtle emotional cues and nonverbal signals that convey the underlying feelings and moods of individuals. It transcends logical reasoning and verbal communication, allowing individuals to intuitively grasp the emotional nuances of a situation and respond empathetically to the needs of others.

Individuals with strong affective intuition possess a heightened sensitivity to emotional dynamics and can accurately discern the feelings of others, even in the absence of explicit verbal expressions. They may intuitively pick up on changes in body language, facial expressions, tone of voice, and other nonverbal cues that convey emotional states, enabling them to empathize with others and offer support and understanding.

Affective intuition plays a crucial role in interpersonal relationships, facilitating deeper connections and fostering empathy and compassion. Individuals who are adept at reading emotional cues and responding empathetically are better equipped to build trust, resolve conflicts, and nurture meaningful connections with others.

Furthermore, affective intuition can guide individuals in making decisions that are aligned with their emotional well-being and values. By tuning into their intuitive sense of how a particular choice or course of action resonates with their emotions, individuals can make decisions that feel authentic and fulfilling, leading to greater overall satisfaction and well-being.

Developing affective intuition involves cultivating self-awareness, empathy, and emotional intelligence. It requires individuals to tune into their own emotions, recognize their impact on others, and develop the ability to empathize with the feelings of those around them. Practices such as mindfulness meditation, reflective journaling, and active listening can help individuals deepen their emotional awareness and strengthen their affective intuition over time.

Interconnectedness of Different Types of Intuition

While the TIS categorizes intuition into distinct types, it's essential to recognize that these types are not mutually exclusive. In reality, intuition is a multifaceted phenomenon that often involves the interplay of various cognitive processes. Holistic, inferential, and affective intuition are interconnected and complementary, working together to inform our decisions and perceptions. By acknowledging the interconnectedness of different types of intuition, you can gain a more holistic understanding of our intuitive abilities.

Take a moment to reflect on your own intuitive tendencies and preferences. Consider which types of intuition resonate most with your own experiences and decision-making processes. Are you more inclined toward holistic thinking, analyzing information logically, or relying on gut feelings and emotions? By engaging in self-reflection and introspection, you can gain valuable insights into your intuitive strengths and areas for growth. This self-awareness empowers you to make more informed choices and leverage your intuitive abilities to achieve your goals and aspirations.

Example Illustrating TIS

Imagine you're deciding whether to accept a job offer. Your gut feeling tells you it's the right move, even though you can't explain why. This is an example of holistic intuition, where you simply "know" without conscious reasoning.

Now, let's say you're evaluating the financial details of the offer, and something feels off. You can't pinpoint the issue, but your subconscious processing of the information is signaling caution. This is an example of analytic intuition, where your mind is processing data below the surface of conscious awareness.

Next, consider receiving feedback from colleagues about the company culture, and you immediately feel a sense of unease or excitement. This is an example of affective intuition, where your emotions provide valuable insights into the situation.

The Rational Experiential Inventory

Introduction to the Rational Experiential Inventory (REI)

REI, developed by Pacini and Epstein in 1999, offers a structured approach to understanding one's cognitive preferences. By assessing the balance between rational and experiential thinking styles, the REI provides valuable insights into how individuals approach decision-making processes. This inventory serves as a helpful tool for personal development, allowing individuals to gain greater self-awareness and make more informed choices in various aspects of their lives. Through its assessment, individuals can identify their cognitive strengths and areas for improvement, paving the way for enhanced decision-making and problem-solving skills.

Explanation of Rational Thinking

Rational thinking is characterized by logical reasoning, evidence-based analysis, and deliberate decision-making processes. Individuals who predominantly rely on rational thinking tend to evaluate information objectively, weigh the pros and cons of different options, and make decisions based on logical principles. This cognitive style emphasizes the importance of empirical evidence and systematic analysis in reaching conclusions. Rational thinkers excel in fields that require analytical skills, such as science, mathematics, and finance, where logical reasoning is essential for problem-solving and decision-making.

Explanation of Experiential Thinking

Experiential thinking involves intuitive processing, reliance on gut feelings, and subconscious pattern recognition. Individuals with a strong preference for experiential thinking trust their instincts and rely on intuition to guide their decisions. This cognitive style emphasizes the importance of emotional intelligence and subconscious processing in decision-making. Experiential thinkers thrive in fields such as psychology, counseling, and creative arts, where empathy, intuition, and creativity play key roles in understanding human behavior and generating innovative ideas.

Assessment of Rational and Experiential Thinking

REI assesses an individual's balance between rational and experiential thinking styles through a series of questions and scenarios. It measures cognitive preferences related to logical reasoning, analytical thinking, intuition, and reliance on gut feelings. By analyzing the responses, the inventory provides insights into how individuals approach decision-making and problem-solving tasks and identifies their cognitive strengths and areas for improvement. This assessment serves as a valuable tool for personal development, allowing individuals to understand their cognitive preferences and leverage them effectively in various situations.

Implications for Decision-Making

Understanding one's cognitive preferences has significant implications for decision-making and problem-solving. Individuals with a balanced approach may benefit from integrating both rational and intuitive thinking styles in their decision-making process. By leveraging both cognitive approaches, they can make more well-rounded decisions that take into account both logical reasoning and intuitive insights. This integrative approach leads to more effective outcomes and greater satisfaction in various areas of their lives, as individuals can leverage the strengths of both cognitive styles to navigate complex situations and challenges successfully.

Importance of Self-Reflection

Understanding your cognitive preferences and thinking styles is crucial for personal evolution. By acknowledging the impact these preferences have on your decision-making, you unlock a pathway to deeper self-awareness and informed choices. Through introspection, you uncover your cognitive strengths and areas ripe for enhancement, enabling the creation of tailored strategies for adeptly harnessing these preferences in diverse scenarios. This reflective journey becomes a springboard for personal development, equipping you with the confidence and resilience needed to navigate life's complexities with poise.

Example Illustrating the REI

Two friends, Alex and Sarah, excitedly plan a vacation together. Alex meticulously thinks about every detail, spending hours comparing flights, scouring hotel reviews, and creating a jam-packed itinerary. His approach is methodical, driven by a desire for certainty and control over every aspect of the trip. Meanwhile, Sarah takes a more spontaneous approach. Without hesitation, she books the first affordable flight she finds and opts to leave the rest of the planning to chance, confident that things will work out as they go.

As the vacation unfolds, they encounter a series of unexpected challenges. A sudden flight cancellation throws a wrench into their plans, leaving them stranded at the airport. While Alex remains composed, quickly consulting their backup options and contacting customer service, Sarah approaches the situation with a sense of adaptability and optimism. Rather than panicking, she suggests exploring nearby attractions while they wait for a resolution.

Throughout their journey, Alex's careful planning proves invaluable in navigating obstacles and ensuring a smooth experience. Yet Sarah's willingness to embrace uncertainty and go with the flow allows them to discover hidden gems and unexpected adventures along the way.

In reflecting on their differing approaches, Alex and Sarah gain insight into their respective cognitive styles. Alex's preference for systematic analysis and preparedness is tempered by Sarah's spontaneity and flexibility, highlighting the complementary nature of their cognitive strengths. Ultimately, their shared experiences deepen their understanding of each other and themselves, enriching their friendship and enhancing their personal growth.

Myers-Briggs Type Indicator

Introduction to the Myers-Briggs Type Indicator (MBTI)

MBTI is a widely recognized personality assessment tool developed by Katharine Cook Briggs and her daughter Isabel Briggs Myers. The MBTI is based on Carl Jung's theory of psychological types and is designed to categorize individuals into one of sixteen personality types. It provides insights into an individual's preferences in how they perceive the world, gather information, make decisions, and interact with others. By understanding their MBTI type, individuals can gain valuable insights into their strengths, weaknesses, communication styles, and preferred ways of approaching various situations. This self-awareness can be instrumental in personal growth, career development, and improving interpersonal relationships.

The MBTI Framework

The MBTI framework is based on four dichotomies, each representing different aspects of personality preferences. These dichotomies include extraversion (E) vs. introversion (I), sensing (S) vs. intuition (N), thinking

(T) vs. feeling (F), and judging (J) vs. perceiving (P). By combining these four dichotomies, the MBTI generates sixteen unique personality types, each characterized by distinct patterns of behavior, cognitive preferences, and interpersonal dynamics. Understanding the MBTI framework provides individuals with a structured way to explore and understand their own personality type, as well as those of others, leading to improved self-awareness and more effective communication and collaboration.

Intuition Dichotomy

The sensing vs. intuition dichotomy in the MBTI framework reflects individuals' preferences in how they gather information and perceive the world. Those with a preference for sensing (S) tend to focus on concrete facts, details, and present realities, relying on their five senses to gather information. In contrast, individuals with a preference for intuition (N) are more inclined to focus on abstract patterns, possibilities, and future implications. They rely on intuition, insights, and imagination to interpret information and make decisions, often seeking out innovative solutions and creative alternatives.

Assessment of Intuitive Preferences

The MBTI assesses intuitive preferences through a series of questions designed to measure individuals' cognitive tendencies. Based on their responses, individuals are categorized as either intuitive (N) or sensing (S) types. Intuitive individuals are characterized by their tendency to trust their gut instincts, focus on future possibilities, and seek out patterns and connections in information. By identifying their intuitive preferences, individuals can gain insights into their cognitive strengths and areas for development, helping them make more informed decisions and navigate life's challenges more effectively.

Implications for Decision-Making

Intuitive preferences, as identified by the MBTI, have significant implications for decision-making processes. Individuals with a preference for Intuition may approach decision-making differently from those with sensing preferences. They tend to rely on abstract patterns and future possibilities to inform their choices, often trusting their gut instincts and intuition to guide them. This cognitive approach can lead to innovative solutions and creative problem-solving, enhancing decision-making effectiveness in various contexts. By leveraging their intuitive strengths, individuals can make more holistic decisions that consider both logical reasoning and creative insights.

Example Illustrating MBTI

Alex is outgoing, sociable, and energized by interacting with others. They prefer to brainstorm ideas with a group and enjoy attending social events. This indicates a preference for extraversion (E) over introversion (I).

Sarah, on the other hand, is introspective and reserved and values time alone for reflection. They prefer to work independently and feel drained by large social gatherings. This suggests a preference for introversion (I) over extraversion (E).

When it comes to processing information, Alex tends to focus on concrete details and relies on past experiences to guide decisions. They prefer a step-by-step approach and value practical solutions. This reflects a preference for sensing (S) over intuition (N).

In contrast, Sarah is imaginative and future-oriented and often sees the big picture rather than getting bogged down in specifics. They enjoy brainstorming creative ideas and exploring possibilities. This indicates a preference for intuition (N) over sensing (S).

Moving on to decision-making, Alex tends to prioritize logical analysis and objective criteria when evaluating options. They value fairness and consistency and strive for logical consistency in their choices. This suggests a preference for thinking (T) over feeling (F).

Conversely, Sarah places a high value on empathy, harmony, and considering the impact of decisions on others' feelings. They make decisions based on personal values and strive for harmony in relationships. This indicates a preference for feeling (F) over thinking (T).

Finally, in terms of lifestyle and organization, Alex prefers structure, plans ahead, and feels comfortable with deadlines. He values organization and enjoys making lists to stay on track. This reflects a preference for judging (J) over perceiving (P).

Meanwhile, Sarah tends to be flexible, adaptable, and spontaneous, preferring to keep her options open and enjoy the process rather than focusing on deadlines. She values exploration and prefers to go with the flow. This indicates a preference for perceiving (P) over judging (J).

In this example, Alex's MBTI type might be ESTJ (extraverted, sensing, thinking, judging), while Sarah's MBTI type might be INFP (introverted, intuitive, feeling, perceiving). These personality types provide insights into their preferences, behaviors, and interactions with others.

Reflect on Past Experiences

Reflective practice serves as our compass, guiding us through the labyrinth of our experiences. By looking back on our past instances, particularly those where intuition played a pivotal role, we uncover valuable insights that pave the way for personal growth and transformation.

Self-reflection prompts us to recall specific moments where our intuition led us toward positive outcomes. By revisiting these instances with clarity and honesty, we illuminate the path forward and gain confidence in our intuitive abilities. Through self-reflection, we unearth the gems of insight buried within our past experiences.

As we integrate intuitive insights into our growth journey, we align our decisions with our values and aspirations. Through self-awareness, we navigate life's complexities with clarity and purpose, forging a path that is true to our authentic selves. By embracing intuition as a guiding force, we unlock the doors to a more fulfilling and purposeful existence.

The journey of intuitive discovery is ongoing, and so is our commitment to reflection and growth. We carve out moments in our daily lives for introspection, journaling, and mindfulness practices. Through consistent practice, we deepen our connection to our intuition and create space for new insights to emerge.

Armed with the wisdom gained from our reflective journey, we step confidently into the future, trusting in our intuition to guide us along the way. With each decision we make, we reclaim our agency and empower ourselves to navigate life's challenges with clarity and confidence. By embracing intuition as a trusted ally, we unlock the door to a world of endless possibilities.

Conclusion

This chapter invites you on a journey of self-discovery and introspection, where the true value lies not in the results of external assessments, but in the insights gained through personal reflection. Throughout this chapter, we've explored various assessment tools, each offering a unique perspective on personality and cognitive preferences.

However, it's crucial to remember that no test can fully capture the complexity of human intuition and personality. While these assessments may provide valuable insights, they are just one piece of the puzzle. True self-understanding comes from introspection, reflection, and a willingness to explore the depths of your own psyche.

As you reflect on the results of these assessments, remember that they are not definitive labels but rather tools for self-awareness and growth. Take the time to consider how your intuitive experiences and past successes align with the insights gained from these assessments. Look for patterns, but also embrace the nuances and contradictions that make you uniquely you.

Ultimately, the most valuable test is the one you conduct within yourself. Reflect on past instances where your intuition served you well, and trust in your innate wisdom to guide you forward. Embrace the journey of self-discovery with curiosity and openness, knowing that each insight gained brings you closer to understanding and harnessing the full power of your intuition.

So, as you continue on your journey of self-discovery, remember that you are more than a set of test scores or personality traits. You are a complex and multifaceted individual, capable of infinite growth and transformation. Trust in your intuition, embrace your unique strengths, and let your inner wisdom be your guide in navigating life's challenges and opportunities.

Chapter Three

Dissect Your Dreams

This chapter will focus on the intriguing world of dreams, where reality blurs and our subconscious mind shines. We will embark on a journey of self-discovery as we explore the complex threads of our dreams, revealing the hidden messages and insights they hold.

Dreams have long fascinated and intrigued us, serving as windows into the deepest recesses of our psyche. Within the labyrinth of our dreams, we encounter a variety of symbols, emotions, and narratives that offer profound glimpses into our innermost thoughts, fears, and desires.

But dreams are more than mere figments of imagination; they are rich repositories of wisdom and knowledge, waiting to be explored and deciphered. We will venture into the depths of dreamland, armed with curiosity and introspection, as we dissect the layers of symbolism and meaning embedded within our dreams.

Our exploration begins with an examination of the science of dreams and their role in intuition. We will discuss the workings of the dreaming mind, exploring the potential benefits of journaling our dreams and uncovering the hidden insights they contain.

Next, we will pose thought-provoking questions to our dreams, inviting introspection and reflection. By questioning assumptions, beliefs, and emotions presented in our dreams, we will unlock the deeper layers of our subconscious mind, gaining greater self-awareness and understanding in the process.

Throughout this chapter, we will be guided by curiosity and wonder as we explore the vast landscape of our dreams. Together, we will embark on a transformative journey of self-discovery, unlocking the hidden wisdom of our subconscious mind and gaining profound insights into ourselves and our lives. So, let us venture forth into the realm of dreams, where mysteries await and revelations abound. Welcome to the exploration of dreamland.

Introduction to the Science of Dreams

Overview of Dreaming

Dreaming is a fascinating and enigmatic aspect of human experience, occurring during the rapid eye movement (REM) stage of sleep, as well as during other stages of non-REM sleep. During REM sleep, the brain becomes highly active, resembling the wakeful state in many respects, despite the body being in a state of paralysis. This paradoxical combination of heightened brain activity and muscular immobility characterizes the dreaming state, which has puzzled scientists and philosophers alike for centuries.

Overall, the phenomenon of dreaming remains a subject of ongoing scientific inquiry and debate. While our understanding of the underlying mechanisms and functions of dreams continues to evolve, one thing is clear: dreams offer a window into the complexities of the human mind, providing fertile ground for exploration and discovery in the realm of psychology and neuroscience.

Theories of Dreaming

Understanding the multifaceted nature of dreams requires delving into the diverse array of theories proposed by scientists and scholars over the years. These theories offer various perspectives on the purpose and function of dreams, reflecting the complexity of the human mind and its capacity for imaginative exploration.

One prominent theory suggests that dreams serve a crucial role in memory consolidation and processing. According to this view, dreams act as a mechanism for organizing and integrating new information acquired during waking hours. During REM sleep, neural networks associated with recent experiences are reactivated, allowing for the consolidation of memories and the strengthening of synaptic connections. This hypothesis is supported by research demonstrating a correlation between REM sleep duration and memory retention, as well as the presence of memory-related brain activity during dreaming.

Another theory posits that dreams function as a means of emotional processing and regulation. Dreams often contain vivid and emotionally charged content, reflecting the dreamer's innermost fears, desires, and conflicts. By providing a safe space for the expression and exploration of emotions, dreams may help individuals work through unresolved psychological issues and achieve emotional equilibrium. This theory is supported by studies showing a link between dream content and emotional experiences in waking life, as well as the therapeutic benefits of dream analysis in psychotherapy.

Additionally, some researchers propose that dreams serve a problem-solving function, allowing individuals to creatively generate solutions to waking life problems or dilemmas. Dreams often contain metaphorical imagery and symbolic representations that can be interpreted as insights or solutions to real-world challenges. This theory is supported by anecdotal evidence of individuals deriving inspiration from their dreams, leading to breakthrough discoveries and innovations in various fields.

Despite the diversity of theories surrounding the nature of dreams, one common thread emerges: dreams are a rich and complex tapestry of mental activity, reflecting the intricate workings of the human mind. While the exact function of dreams remains a subject of ongoing debate and inquiry, their significance in shaping our psychological well-being and cognitive processes cannot be overstated.

Dreams and Intuition

Dreams have long been regarded as a portal to the subconscious mind, offering glimpses into our deepest thoughts, emotions, and desires. Within the realm of intuition, dreams play a significant role in guiding individuals toward greater self-awareness and insight.

One way in which dreams intersect with intuition is through the exploration of emotions and unconscious thoughts. Dreams often contain symbolic imagery and narrative themes that reflect the dreamer's innermost fears, desires, and conflicts. By engaging with these symbolic representations, individuals can gain valuable insights into their emotional landscape and subconscious motivations. For example, recurring dreams or dream symbols may indicate unresolved issues or recurring patterns in the dreamer's life, offering clues to areas that may require further exploration or healing.

Additionally, dreams can serve as a source of intuitive wisdom and guidance. Many individuals report experiencing "intuitive dreams" that provide insights or solutions to real-life problems or dilemmas. These dreams may contain metaphorical imagery or symbolic messages that offer perspective or clarity on a particular situation. By paying attention to the intuitive insights conveyed in dreams, individuals can tap into their inner wisdom and make informed decisions in waking life.

Benefits of Journaling Dreams

Increased Self-Awareness

Dream journaling serves as a powerful tool for cultivating self-awareness by prompting individuals to explore the depths of their subconscious mind. Through the act of recording dreams regularly, individuals are encouraged to pay closer attention to their inner thoughts, emotions, and experiences, leading to a deeper understanding of themselves.

One of the primary ways dream journaling enhances self-awareness is by facilitating self-reflection. As individuals recount their dreams and commit them to paper, they engage in a process of introspection, pondering the significance of the dream symbols, narratives, and emotions. This reflective practice prompts individuals to explore the underlying meanings behind their dreams, uncovering hidden aspects of their psyche that may have remained dormant in their waking consciousness.

Dream journaling also provides a platform for individuals to confront and explore their innermost fears, desires, and unresolved conflicts. Dreams often serve as a mirror reflecting the subconscious mind, revealing aspects of the self that may be obscured or repressed in waking life. By documenting dreams and examining their content, individuals gain insight into their deepest motivations, anxieties, and aspirations, fostering a greater sense of self-understanding and acceptance.

Furthermore, the process of dream journaling encourages individuals to identify patterns and recurring themes in their dreams, offering valuable clues to their underlying psychological landscape. By recognizing common motifs, symbols, and storylines in their dreams, individuals gain insight into recurring patterns of thought, emotion, and behavior that may be influencing their waking life. This awareness enables individuals to address unresolved issues, challenge limiting beliefs, and embark on a journey of personal growth and transformation.

Dream journaling, therefore, serves as a pathway to increased self-awareness, empowering individuals to explore the depths of their subconscious mind and uncover the hidden truths within. By engaging in this reflective practice, individuals gain a deeper understanding of themselves, their relationships, and their life's purpose, ultimately leading to greater fulfillment and authenticity in their waking lives.

Emotional Processing

Dream journaling serves as an invaluable tool for emotional processing, offering individuals a safe and cathartic space to explore and navigate their inner emotional landscape. Through the act of recording dreams and reflecting on associated emotions, individuals can gain deeper insight into their feelings, experiences, and psychological well-being.

One of the primary benefits of dream journaling for emotional processing is the opportunity it provides for emotional expression and exploration. Dreams often contain vivid and emotionally charged content, reflecting the dreamer's innermost fears, desires, and conflicts. By writing about dream content and associated emotions, individuals can externalize their feelings and gain perspective on their emotional experiences, leading to a sense of validation and catharsis.

Moreover, dream journaling enables individuals to make sense of their emotions and develop healthier coping mechanisms for dealing with stress, anxiety, and other emotional challenges. By examining the emotional themes and patterns present in their dreams, individuals can identify recurring issues or triggers that may be contributing to emotional distress in their waking life. This allows individuals to proactively address these challenges, seek support when needed, and cultivate greater emotional resilience and well-being.

Dream journaling also offers a unique opportunity for emotional release and healing. Through the process of writing about dream content and associated emotions, individuals can release pent-up emotions, traumas, and unresolved conflicts that may be lingering beneath the surface of their consciousness. This emotional release can provide a sense of relief and closure, allowing individuals to move forward with greater clarity, purpose, and peace of mind.

Dream journaling offers individuals a therapeutic outlet for expressing, exploring, and resolving their innermost feelings. By engaging in this reflective practice, individuals can gain insight into their emotional experiences, develop healthy coping strategies, and cultivate greater emotional resilience and well-being.

Creative Inspiration

Dream journaling is not only a tool for self-reflection and emotional processing but also a source of boundless creative inspiration. By recording and exploring their dreams, individuals can tap into the rich potential of their subconscious mind, unlocking a wealth of imaginative ideas, artistic vision, and problem-solving solutions.

One of the primary ways dream journaling fosters creative inspiration is through the vivid and imaginative imagery often present in dreams. Dreams are known for their surreal landscapes, fantastical creatures, and symbolic motifs, providing fertile ground for creative exploration and expression. By capturing these visual elements in writing or drawing, individuals can translate their dream experiences into works of art, literature, or other creative endeavors.

Moreover, dream journaling encourages individuals to think outside the box and explore unconventional ideas and perspectives. Dreams often defy the constraints of logic and reality, presenting individuals with novel scenarios, alternate realities, and imaginative solutions to complex problems. By embracing the creative freedom of dreams, individuals can expand their creative horizons, experiment with new concepts, and push the boundaries of their artistic expression.

Dreams also serve as a source of inspiration for problem-solving and innovation. Many famous artists, writers, scientists, and inventors throughout history have drawn inspiration from their dreams, leading to groundbreaking discoveries, artistic masterpieces, and technological advancements. By paying attention to the insights and solutions presented in their dreams, individuals can harness the creative power of their subconscious mind to overcome challenges and generate innovative ideas in their waking life.

Furthermore, dream journaling provides a platform for exploring and expressing the deeper themes and emotions present in dreams. By reflecting on the symbolic meaning and underlying messages of their dreams, individuals can infuse their creative projects with greater depth, authenticity, and emotional resonance. This deeper level of engagement with dream content can enrich the creative process, leading to more meaningful and impactful artistic endeavors.

Uncovering Patterns and Themes

Dream journaling serves as a valuable tool for uncovering patterns and themes in one's dreams, offering insight into the subconscious mind and revealing hidden aspects of the self. By recording and reflecting on dream experiences, individuals can identify recurring motifs, symbols, and storylines that provide valuable clues to their underlying psychological landscape.

One of the primary benefits of dream journaling for uncovering patterns and themes is the opportunity it provides for self-exploration and introspection. As individuals document their dreams over time, they may begin to notice common themes or recurring elements that appear across multiple dreams. These patterns may include recurring symbols, settings, characters, or emotional states, which can offer insight into the dreamer's inner thoughts, feelings, and experiences.

Uncovering patterns and themes in dreams can shed light on unresolved issues or recurring challenges in the dreamer's life. By identifying common motifs or storylines that appear in their dreams, individuals can gain insight into underlying psychological themes or conflicts that may be influencing their waking life. This allows individuals to address these issues proactively, seeking resolution and healing where needed.

Dream journaling also provides a platform for exploring the symbolic meaning and significance of dream content. By reflecting on the imagery, symbols, and narrative elements present in their dreams, individuals can decipher the deeper messages and themes embedded within them. This symbolic interpretation can reveal hidden truths, insights, and guidance, guiding individuals toward greater self-understanding and personal growth.

Uncovering patterns and themes in dreams can facilitate the integration of unconscious material into conscious awareness. As individuals recognize and acknowledge recurring patterns in their dreams, they begin to integrate these insights into their waking life, leading to greater clarity, authenticity, and self-acceptance. This process of integration helps for psychological wholeness and alignment, empowering individuals to live more fulfilling and meaningful lives.

Improved Sleep Quality

Engaging in dream journaling as part of a bedtime routine can significantly improve sleep quality and overall well-being. By dedicating time before sleep to reflect on and record the events of the day, individuals can effectively clear their minds of lingering thoughts and emotions, promoting relaxation and mental clarity. This process of "mental decluttering" allows the brain to transition more smoothly into a state of rest, leading to deeper and more restful sleep cycles.

Furthermore, the act of journaling dreams can serve as a form of cognitive closure, helping individuals process any unresolved issues or emotions before bedtime. By externalizing their thoughts and experiences onto paper, individuals may find it easier to let go of stressors and worries, creating a more conducive environment for sleep.

In addition to improving sleep quality, dream journaling can also enhance dream recall and awareness. As individuals become more attuned to their dreams and the messages they contain, they may develop a greater sense of connection to their inner selves and subconscious mind.

Overall, incorporating dream journaling into a nightly routine can have profound benefits for both mental and physical well-being. By nurturing a deeper understanding of their dreams and inner experiences, individuals can cultivate a greater sense of self-awareness, emotional resilience, and overall vitality.

Exploring Dream Questions

Introduction to Dream Questioning

Dream questioning serves as a gateway to unlocking the deeper layers of the subconscious mind and offers a pathway to profound self-discovery and introspection. By embracing the practice of asking thought-provoking questions, individuals can dive beneath the surface of their dreams, revealing hidden insights and truths that may elude conscious awareness.

The essence of dream questioning lies in its ability to challenge assumptions, beliefs, and emotions presented in dreams, opening the door to a deeper understanding of the self. Rather than passively accepting the narrative of our dreams, we are encouraged to approach them with a curious and critical mindset, questioning the underlying messages and symbolism they contain.

Through the process of dream questioning, individuals can uncover layers of meaning and significance that may have gone unnoticed, leading to profound revelations and moments of clarity. By interrogating the content of our dreams, we can peel back the layers of the subconscious mind, exposing hidden fears, desires, and unresolved conflicts that shape our waking lives.

Thought-Provoking Questions

In the exploration of dreams, the art of asking the right questions is crucial. Thought-provoking questions help individuals navigate through the labyrinth of their dreamscape, unraveling layers of symbolism and meaning. These questions, when posed with intention and curiosity, prompt introspection and unlock the hidden insights embedded within dreams.

Thought-provoking questions help us explore various aspects of dream content, emotions, symbols, and themes, igniting the flames of self-discovery. Questions such as "What emotions did the dream evoke?" prompt individuals to explore the emotional landscape of their dreams, uncovering underlying feelings and motivations. By delving into the emotional resonance of their dreams, individuals gain deeper insight into their innermost desires, fears, and conflicts, fostering emotional intelligence and self-awareness.

Similarly, questions that focus on recurring symbols or themes in dreams encourage individuals to recognize patterns and motifs that may hold significant meaning. Asking "What recurring symbols or themes appeared in the dream?" prompts reflection on the symbolic language of dreams, uncovering hidden messages and insights. Through the exploration of recurring symbols, individuals can decipher the deeper meaning behind their dreams, gaining clarity and understanding.

Moreover, thought-provoking questions invite individuals to consider the relationship between their dreams and waking life experiences. Questions such as "What aspects of my waking life might this dream be reflecting?" bridge the gap between the dream world and reality, facilitating integration and self-reflection. By examining the parallels between dreams and waking life, individuals can gain valuable insights into their subconscious thoughts and behaviors, paving the way for personal growth and transformation.

Thought-provoking questions serve as the cornerstone of dream exploration, guiding individuals on a journey of self-discovery and introspection. Through the practice of asking these questions, individuals can unlock the hidden wisdom of their dreams, gaining profound insights into their innermost thoughts, emotions, and experiences.

Practical Application of Dream Questioning

The practical application of dream questioning bridges the gap between theory and action, empowering individuals to integrate this transformative practice into their daily lives. By adopting practical strategies for incorporating dream questioning, individuals can harness the power of introspection and self-exploration to unlock the hidden insights within their dreams.

One practical strategy for applying dream questioning is the establishment of a dedicated dream journal. By recording dreams regularly and reflecting on their content, individuals create a tangible record of their dream experiences, facilitating deeper exploration and analysis. Journaling encourages active engagement with dreams, prompting individuals to ask thought-provoking questions and uncover hidden insights.

Additionally, individuals can leverage reflective exercises to deepen their understanding of dream content and symbolism. Reflective exercises, such as visualization or meditation, create a space for quiet contemplation and introspection, allowing individuals to connect with the deeper layers of their subconscious mind. By incorporating these practices into their daily routine, individuals can cultivate a deeper awareness of their dreams and unlock their transformative potential.

Moreover, dream questioning can be integrated into daily rituals and routines, such as morning reflection or bedtime meditation. By setting aside dedicated time for introspection and dream exploration, individuals create a structured framework for engaging with their dreams and uncovering hidden insights. These daily rituals serve as anchors, grounding individuals in the practice of dream questioning and fostering a deeper connection with their subconscious mind.

Conclusion

As we draw to a close on our journey through the labyrinth of dreams, we are left with a profound appreciation for the depth and complexity of the human psyche. In dissecting our dreams, we have uncovered hidden truths, explored the depths of our subconscious mind, and gained invaluable insights into ourselves and our lives.

Throughout this chapter, we have witnessed the transformative power of dream exploration, from the science of dreams to the practical application of dream questioning. We have learned that dreams are not merely fleeting images that vanish with the morning light but profound reflections of our innermost thoughts, emotions, and experiences.

By journaling our dreams, we have created a tangible record of our subconscious mind, allowing us to delve deeper into the layers of symbolism and meaning that lie beneath the surface. Through the art of dream questioning, we have challenged assumptions, beliefs, and emotions, opening the door to greater self-awareness and understanding.

But our journey does not end here. As we bid farewell to the realm of dreams, we carry with us a newfound appreciation for the wisdom that lies within. Our dreams are a constant source of guidance and offer insights and revelations that can illuminate our path forward.

So, as we return to the waking world, let us carry with us the lessons learned in dreamland. Let us continue to explore, question, and reflect, for in doing so, we unlock the door to a deeper understanding of ourselves and the world around us.

Chapter Four

Be Conscious of the Subconscious

Welcome to Chapter 4, where we delve deep into the fascinating realm of the subconscious mind and its pivotal role in shaping our lives. In this chapter, we will explore the enigmatic nature of intuition and its profound influence on human cognition and decision-making processes.

The subconscious mind, often described as a hidden reservoir of wisdom, operates beneath the surface of conscious awareness, processing vast amounts of information and guiding our actions in ways we may not fully understand. Through the lens of dual process theory, we will dissect the intricacies of intuitive thinking, distinguishing between the rapid, automatic responses of System 1 and the deliberate, analytical processes of System 2.

We will uncover the mechanisms of intuitive learning systems, exploring how our minds absorb, process, and store information without conscious awareness. By understanding the dynamics of these intuitive processes, we gain insight into how our subconscious minds shape our perceptions, judgments, and decision-making abilities. Intuitive learning systems, deeply entrenched in the subconscious mind, form the foundation for System 1 processes, characterized by rapid, automatic responses driven by heuristics and pattern recognition. These systems, continuously operating without conscious awareness, play a pivotal role in shaping human cognition and decision-making.

Furthermore, cultivating awareness becomes essential in navigating the potential biases and distortions inherent in intuitive learning systems. By fostering mindfulness and self-reflection, individuals can attune themselves to the subtle cues emanating from their subconscious minds. Simultaneously, the dual processing theory distinguishes System 2, a slower and deliberate cognitive process, which requires conscious effort and analytical reasoning. Understanding this interplay sheds light on how awareness contributes to navigating the complexities of intuitive learning systems, thereby enhancing the overall decision-making process by integrating both spontaneous and deliberate cognitive functions.

Throughout this chapter, we will emphasize the importance of awareness in mastering the power of intuition. Through mindfulness practices, self-reflection, and critical thinking, we can cultivate a deeper understanding of our intuitive insights and mitigate the biases that may distort our judgments.

The Nature of Intuition

The Subconscious Mind

The subconscious mind, a realm of mystery and intrigue, plays a profound role in shaping human behavior and cognition. Operating beneath the surface of conscious awareness, it processes vast amounts of information, influences our perceptions, and guides our actions in ways that often go unnoticed. Understanding the workings of the subconscious mind is crucial for unraveling the mysteries of intuition and unlocking its transformative potential.

Central to the exploration of intuition is the concept of dual processing theory, which posits that human cognition operates on two distinct levels: System 1 and System 2. System 1, often associated with intuition, is fast, automatic, and operates largely outside of conscious awareness. It relies on heuristics, or mental shortcuts, to make rapid judgments and decisions based on pattern recognition and past experiences. In contrast, System 2 is slower, deliberate, and requires conscious effort. It engages in rational analysis, logical reasoning, and problem-solving, drawing upon conscious awareness and cognitive resources.

The subconscious mind predominantly drives System 1 processing, serving as the engine behind our intuitive responses and automatic behaviors. It effortlessly sifts through vast amounts of sensory information, identifies patterns, and generates intuitive insights without conscious effort. This subconscious processing allows us to navigate the complexities of everyday life with remarkable efficiency, making split-second decisions and judgments with ease.

Yet the subconscious mind is not infallible. It is susceptible to distortions and errors that can cloud our judgment and lead to irrational decision-making. Subconscious beliefs and cultural influences can shape our intuitive responses, leading to cognitive biases such as confirmation bias, availability bias, and anchoring bias. These biases can distort our perceptions, reinforce stereotypes, and undermine the accuracy of our intuitive judgments. They will be discussed later in a greater detail in a section titled Overcome Intuitive Bias.

Despite its imperfections, the subconscious mind serves as a powerful reservoir of intuitive wisdom, offering insights and understandings that transcend the limitations of conscious thought. By exploring the workings of the subconscious mind, we can gain a deeper understanding of intuition and harness its transformative potential. Cultivating mindfulness, self-awareness, and critical thinking skills can help us navigate the complexities of intuitive processing, enhancing our decision-making abilities and fostering greater clarity and insight in our lives.

Intuitive Learning Systems

Intuitive learning systems represent the network of processes through which our minds absorb, process, and store information without conscious awareness. These systems operate continuously, tirelessly accumulating experiences, insights, and beliefs that shape our perceptions, judgments, and decision-making abilities. Understanding the dynamics of intuitive learning systems is essential for unraveling the mysteries of intuition and tapping into its transformative power.

At the heart of intuitive learning systems lies the subconscious mind, a vast reservoir of knowledge and wisdom that operates beneath the surface of conscious awareness. This subconscious processing enables us to absorb information, often without consciously registering the stimuli around us. Whether it's learning to ride a bicycle, recognizing familiar faces, or deciphering complex social cues, intuitive learning systems play a crucial role in shaping our understanding of the world.

One of the remarkable features of intuitive learning systems is their adaptability and flexibility. These systems are not static repositories of information but dynamic processes that evolve and adapt over time. They incorporate new experiences, update existing beliefs, and refine our understanding of the world in response to changing circumstances. This adaptive capacity allows us to learn from our mistakes, refine our skills, and navigate novel situations with confidence and ease.

However, intuitive learning systems are not immune to biases and distortions. These biases can manifest in various forms, such as confirmation bias, where we seek out information that confirms our existing beliefs, or availability bias, where we overestimate the significance of information that is readily available in memory.

Despite these challenges, cultivating awareness and mindfulness can help us navigate the complexities of intuitive learning systems more effectively. By becoming attuned to subconscious cues and intuitions, we can gain insight into our thought processes, recognize potential biases, and make more informed decisions. Practices such as meditation, journaling, and reflective thinking can enhance our self-awareness and foster a deeper understanding of the workings of our intuitive minds.

In essence, understanding intuitive learning systems offers a window into the fascinating interplay between conscious and subconscious processes in shaping human cognition. By unraveling the mysteries of intuition and honing our awareness of intuitive learning systems, we can unlock new dimensions of insight, creativity, and understanding in our lives.

Importance of Awareness

Cultivating awareness is essential for mastering the power of intuition and unlocking its transformative potential. In a world inundated with distractions and stimuli, mindfulness and self-awareness can provide a gateway to deeper insights and understanding.

Mindfulness, often described as the practice of being present in the moment without judgment, lies at the heart of cultivating awareness. By cultivating mindfulness, individuals can sharpen their focus, enhance their attention, and become more attuned to the subtle cues and signals emanating from their subconscious minds. Through practices such as meditation, deep breathing, and body scanning, individuals can cultivate a heightened sense of awareness and presence, enabling them to tap into their intuitive insights more effectively.

Self-awareness is another crucial component of cultivating awareness. By developing a deeper understanding of one's thoughts, emotions, and behaviors, individuals can gain insight into the workings of their subconscious minds and recognize patterns and tendencies that may influence their intuitive responses. Self-awareness enables individuals to identify potential biases, assumptions, and limiting beliefs that may cloud their judgment and impede their ability to make informed decisions.

Practical strategies can help individuals become more attuned to subconscious cues and intuitions in their daily lives. Journaling, for example, can serve as a powerful tool for self-reflection, enabling individuals to track their thoughts, emotions, and experiences over time. By recording their intuitive hunches, gut feelings, and insights, individuals can gain valuable insights into the workings of their intuitive minds and discern patterns and trends that may inform their decision-making processes.

Moreover, engaging in reflective practices, such as contemplation and introspection, can deepen one's understanding of intuitive insights and their underlying motivations. By setting aside time for quiet reflection and introspection, individuals can create space for intuitive insights to emerge and flourish, unencumbered by the noise and distractions of everyday life.

The Dual Process Theory

The dual process theory of thinking provides a framework for understanding the two distinct modes of thought that govern human cognition: System 1 and System 2. These systems operate in tandem, each contributing unique strengths and characteristics to the decision-making process.

System 1 (Intuition)

System 1, often referred to as intuition, is characterized by its automaticity and rapidity. It operates effortlessly and spontaneously, generating quick judgments and responses based on heuristics, or mental shortcuts. Intuitive thinking is driven by patterns, associations, and past experiences stored in the subconscious mind, allowing individuals to make split-second decisions without conscious deliberation. Instead of engaging in conscious deliberation, heuristics allow individuals to make rapid judgments and responses effortlessly. In the context of catching a ball, for instance, heuristics facilitate automatic adjustments of body movements based on ingrained motor skills and spatial awareness, without the need for conscious calculation of trajectory or force.

For example, consider the example of catching a ball thrown toward you. In this scenario, you don't consciously calculate the trajectory of the ball or the force needed to catch it. Instead, your intuitive system automatically adjusts your body's movements to intercept the ball, relying on ingrained motor skills and spatial awareness to accomplish the task.

System 2 (Deliberative)

In contrast to the automaticity of System 1, System 2 operates through conscious effort and deliberation. It involves analytical reasoning, logical thinking, and cognitive processing that require conscious attention and cognitive resources. System 2 is slower and more deliberate than System 1, often employed when faced with complex or novel situations that demand careful consideration and problem-solving.

To illustrate System 2 in action, imagine solving a mathematical problem or evaluating competing options for a major life decision. These tasks require conscious thought, concentration, and mental effort as you systematically weigh the pros and cons, analyze information, and arrive at a reasoned conclusion.

Interaction between the Two Systems

The interaction between System 1 and System 2 is dynamic and complex, with each system influencing and complementing the other in decision-making scenarios. While System 1 provides rapid, intuitive responses to familiar situations, System 2 serves as a check on automatic responses, allowing for deeper analysis and reflection when necessary.

In many cases, intuitive judgments made by System 1 serve as valuable heuristics, guiding initial impressions and informing subsequent deliberations by System 2. However, System 2 may also override intuitive responses when they lead to biased or suboptimal decisions, engaging in more thorough analysis and rational deliberation to arrive at a more reasoned conclusion.

Understanding the interaction between these two systems is crucial for making informed decisions and navigating the complexities of everyday life. By recognizing the strengths and limitations of both intuition and analytical thinking, individuals can leverage the complementary nature of System 1 and System 2 to enhance their decision-making abilities and achieve optimal outcomes.

The Power of Intuition

Practical Tips for Intuitive Insights

Here are some practical strategies to harness the power of intuition in your daily life:

- **Mindfulness Practices**: Engage in mindfulness meditation, yoga, or mindful breathing exercises to cultivate present-moment awareness. These practices help quiet the chatter of the mind and create space for intuitive insights to emerge.

- **Body Awareness**: Pay attention to bodily sensations and cues, such as tightness in the chest or a fluttering feeling in the stomach. Your body often communicates intuitive messages that can guide your decisions and actions.

- **Journaling and Reflection**: Keep a journal to record your intuitive hunches, dreams, and synchronicities. Reflect on these entries regularly to discern patterns, themes, and insights that may offer valuable guidance from your subconscious mind.

- **Creative Expression**: Engage in creative activities such as painting, writing, or playing music to tap into your intuitive creativity. Allow yourself to explore without judgment or expectation, trusting that your intuition will guide you toward authentic self-expression.

- **Nature Immersion**: Spend time in nature, whether it's a walk in the park, a hike in the mountains, or a day at the beach. Nature has a way of quieting the mind and connecting us to our intuitive senses, allowing for greater clarity and insight.

- **Silent Reflection**: Set aside time each day for silent reflection or contemplation. Whether it's through meditation, prayer, or simply sitting in quiet solitude, these moments of stillness can help you connect with your inner wisdom and intuition.

- **Trust and Act**: Practice trusting your intuition by acting on small hunches or gut feelings in everyday situations. Start with low-stakes decisions and observe the outcomes. Over time, as you see positive results from following your intuition, you'll develop greater confidence in its guidance.

Intuition in Creative Endeavors

Creativity and intuition share a symbiotic relationship, each fueling and inspiring the other. Intuition manifests in many forms when it comes to creative endeavors:

- **Inspiration and Insight**: Intuition often serves as the wellspring of creative inspiration, providing artists, writers, and innovators with sudden flashes of insight or breakthrough ideas. By tapping into their intuitive minds, creatives can access a rich reservoir of imaginative possibilities.

- **Embracing Uncertainty**: Creative endeavors frequently involve navigating uncertainty and ambiguity, where there are no clear-cut answers or formulas for success. Intuition enables creatives to embrace uncertainty, trust their instincts, and explore uncharted territory with confidence.

- **Flow State**: Intuitive creativity often arises in a state of flow, where individuals are fully immersed in the creative process and lose track of time and self-consciousness. In this heightened state of awareness, intuitive insights flow freely, leading to moments of creative brilliance.

- **Synchronicity and Serendipity**: Intuition fosters a mindset of openness and receptivity to serendipitous encounters, chance connections, and unexpected discoveries. By remaining attuned to intuitive nudges and synchronicities, creatives can harness the magic of serendipity in their work.

- **Problem-Solving**: Creativity requires thinking outside the box and finding innovative solutions to challenges. Intuition can play a crucial role in problem-solving by providing subtle insights and unconventional ideas that may not be immediately obvious through logical analysis alone.

- **Decision-Making**: Intuition can help creative individuals make decisions by tapping into their inner wisdom and trusting their instincts. Whether choosing between artistic directions or deciding on the final edits of a piece, intuition often guides creators toward choices that feel authentic and aligned with their vision.

- **Emotional Expression**: Creativity is often a means of emotional expression, allowing individuals to channel their feelings into their work. Intuition can act as a conduit for these emotions, helping artists tap into deeper layers of experience and convey them authentically through their creative endeavors.

- **Exploration and Discovery**: Intuition encourages creative exploration and experimentation, leading artists to explore new techniques, themes, and mediums. By following their intuition, creators can push past boundaries, break new ground, and make unexpected discoveries in their artistic practice.

- **Connection to Audience**: Intuition can also help creators connect with their audience on a deeper level. By trusting their instincts and staying true to their unique vision, artists can create work that resonates with others and evokes a powerful emotional response.

Throughout history, countless artists, writers, and inventors have relied on intuitive insights to fuel their creative endeavors. Vincent van Gogh famously trusted his intuition when applying bold brushstrokes to his canvases, while Mozart credited his compositions to intuitive melodies that seemed to flow effortlessly from his mind. Similarly, innovators like Steve Jobs and Albert Einstein trusted their intuition to guide them toward groundbreaking discoveries and inventions.

By recognizing the integral role of intuition in creative expression, individuals can cultivate their intuitive abilities and unlock their creative potential to make meaningful contributions to the world. Whether through art, music, writing, or innovation, intuition serves as a guiding light, illuminating the path to deeper self-expression and connection.

Overcome Intuitive Biases

Common Biases in Intuitive Thinking

Intuitive thinking, while often efficient and effective, can also be prone to biases and pitfalls that distort our judgments and decisions. Here are some common biases associated with intuitive decision-making:

- **Confirmation Bias**: This bias occurs when individuals seek out information that confirms their existing beliefs or hypotheses while ignoring contradictory evidence. For example, a manager may only focus on positive performance metrics when evaluating an employee they already perceive as competent, overlooking signs of underperformance.

- **Availability Bias**: The availability bias occurs when individuals overestimate the likelihood of events or outcomes based on their ease of recall from memory. For instance, people may perceive air travel as more dangerous than driving, despite statistical evidence suggesting otherwise, because plane crashes receive more media coverage and are, therefore, more salient in memory.

- **Anchoring Bias**: Anchoring bias occurs when individuals rely too heavily on the first piece of information encountered (the "anchor") when making decisions. For instance, a real estate agent might suggest a higher selling price for a property based on the initial asking price, even if market conditions suggest a lower valuation.

- **Overconfidence Bias**: This bias involves an inflated sense of confidence in one's judgments or abilities, leading individuals to overestimate their accuracy or likelihood of success. For example, a trader may believe they have a special knack for predicting market movements, leading them to take excessive risks without adequately assessing potential downsides.

- **Representativeness Heuristic**: The tendency to make judgments or decisions based on how closely an object or situation resembles a prototype or stereotype. This can lead to errors in judgment when individuals rely too heavily on superficial similarities without considering other relevant factors. Imagine someone assuming that a person wearing glasses must be highly intelligent because they fit the stereotype of a "nerd" or "intellectual," without considering other factors such as individual capabilities or interests.

- **Hindsight Bias**: The tendency to perceive past events as having been more predictable than they actually were. This bias can lead individuals to believe that they knew or should have known the outcome of an event based on their current knowledge or beliefs. For example, After a stock market crash, someone might claim they "knew all along" that it was going to happen, even if they didn't predict it beforehand. This bias leads them to believe that the event was more predictable than it actually was.

- **Emotional Bias**: The influence of emotions on intuitive thinking, which can lead individuals to make decisions based on feelings rather than rational analysis. This bias can result in decisions that are influenced by fear, excitement, or other strong emotions rather than objective evidence or logic. For instance, an investor might make impulsive decisions to buy or sell stocks based on their fear of losing money during market fluctuations instead of following a rational investment strategy based on long-term goals and market analysis.

Strategies for Bias Mitigation

While biases are inherent to human cognition, there are strategies we can employ to recognize and mitigate their influence on intuitive thinking:

- **Awareness and Reflection**: Cultivate awareness of your own cognitive biases by reflecting on past decisions and considering alternative perspectives. Actively question your assumptions and beliefs to uncover potential biases that may be influencing your thinking.

- **Seek Diverse Perspectives**: Encourage diversity of thought and perspectives within decision-making processes to counteract the effects of groupthink and confirmation bias. Consult with individuals who offer different viewpoints and challenge your assumptions to ensure a more comprehensive evaluation of options.

- **Utilize Decision-Making Frameworks**: Adopt decision-making frameworks such as the "premortem" technique, where you imagine that a decision has already failed and work backward to identify potential pitfalls and biases. This approach can help uncover blind spots and mitigate the influence of overconfidence bias.

- **Practice Critical Thinking**: Develop your critical thinking skills by questioning assumptions, evaluating evidence objectively, and weighing alternative interpretations. Avoid making snap judgments based on gut feelings alone and instead engage in systematic analysis and evaluation of information.

- **Embrace Skepticism**: Maintain a healthy dose of skepticism toward intuitive judgments and claims, recognizing that intuition is not infallible and may be influenced by biases and heuristics. Approach decisions with an open mind and a willingness to challenge your own assumptions and beliefs.

By implementing these strategies, individuals can enhance their ability to recognize and mitigate biases in intuitive thinking, leading to more informed and objective decision-making processes. While biases may never be entirely eliminated, cultivating awareness and employing critical thinking techniques can help minimize their impact and improve the quality of intuitive judgments and decisions.

Further Reading or Resources

If you are interested in delving deeper into the topic of intuition and subconscious processing, the following books and resources are recommended:

- *Thinking, Fast and Slow* by Daniel Kahneman: The book explores the two systems of thinking and delves into the cognitive biases that influence our decision-making processes.

- *Blink: The Power of Thinking without Thinking* by Malcolm Gladwell: Gladwell examines the power of intuition and rapid cognition, highlighting the ways in which snap judgments can be both insightful and deceptive.

- *The Power of Intuition: How to Use Your Gut Feelings to Make Better Decisions at Work* by Gary Klein: Klein explores the role of intuition in decision-making, drawing on insights from psychology, neuroscience, and real-world examples.

- *Intuition: Knowing beyond Logic* by Osho: This book offers a philosophical perspective on intuition, encouraging readers to trust their inner wisdom and intuition as a guide to living a more fulfilling life.

- *The Intuitive Way: The Definitive Guide to Increasing Your Awareness* by Penney Peirce: Peirce provides practical exercises and techniques for developing intuition and expanding awareness in daily life.

Conclusion

In this chapter, we explored the fascinating realm of intuition and its profound impact on human cognition and decision-making. We discussed the nature of intuition as the innate ability to understand or know something instinctively, without the need for conscious reasoning. Through an exploration of the dual process theory, we distinguished between System 1 (intuition) and System 2 (deliberative) processes, highlighting the automaticity of intuitive thinking and the conscious effort required for analytical reasoning.

We delved into the workings of the subconscious mind, uncovering its role in shaping intuitive processing and accumulating information and beliefs without conscious awareness. From understanding intuitive learning systems to cultivating awareness through mindfulness and self-reflection, we explored practical strategies for tapping into intuitive insights in daily life.

We also examined the pivotal role of intuition in creative endeavors, illustrating how intuitive insights fuel innovation, problem-solving, and artistic expression. Through examples of renowned artists, writers, and inventors, we witnessed the transformative power of intuition in unleashing creative potential and fostering breakthroughs.

However, we also explored the inherent biases and pitfalls associated with intuitive thinking, such as confirmation bias, availability bias, and overconfidence bias. Recognizing these biases is crucial for making informed decisions and avoiding errors in judgment.

To sum it up, intuition is a valuable resource that can be cultivated and refined through awareness and practice. By embracing our intuitive abilities and trusting our instincts, we can enhance our decision-making, problem-solving, and creative endeavors. However, it's essential to remain vigilant against potential biases and errors that may distort our intuitive judgments. By cultivating awareness, practicing critical thinking, and seeking diverse perspectives, we can harness the full potential of intuition while mitigating its limitations.

Chapter Five

Work with Your Intuition

In this chapter, we discuss proactive engagement with intuition, understanding how to harness its power and integrate it into our lives.

Intuition is not a mysterious force reserved for a select few; it is a skill that can be cultivated and refined by anyone willing to put in the effort. We'll explore the concept of intuition as a developable skill, understanding how conscious practice and effort play crucial roles in honing our intuitive abilities.

We'll uncover the potential within each of us to nurture and refine our intuitive abilities. From recognizing direct intuitive signals to understanding the subtleties of indirect intuition, we'll equip you with the tools and insights necessary to embrace intuition as a guiding force in decision-making and problem-solving.

Throughout this chapter, we'll navigate the challenges and doubts that may arise on this journey, offering strategies to overcome skepticism and resistance. Through real-life examples and practical techniques, we'll illuminate the path toward harnessing the full potential of your intuition.

You Can Develop Intuition

Intuition as a Developable Skill

Intuition is often viewed as an innate ability, but research suggests that it is a skill that can be cultivated and refined over time. Studies, such as those conducted by Lieberman (2000), indicate a trajectory of improvement in intuitive abilities from childhood to adulthood. This developmental pattern suggests that intuition is not solely dependent on genetic predispositions but is influenced by environmental factors, learning experiences, and cognitive maturation. Throughout their lives, individuals encounter various situations that prompt them to rely on their intuitive faculties, gradually honing their ability to perceive subtle cues, patterns, and insights.

The finding that intuition improves with age carries profound implications for the learnability and development of intuitive abilities. It suggests that intuitive skills are not solely dependent on inherent traits but can be nurtured and strengthened through deliberate practice and exposure to diverse experiences.

This understanding challenges the misconception that intuition is fixed and unchangeable and offers hope and encouragement to those who seek to enhance their intuitive capacities. When they recognize intuition as a developable skill, individuals can approach it with a growth mindset and embrace opportunities for learning, practice, and self-improvement.

The Role of Conscious Effort and Practice

While intuition may naturally evolve with age, its development can be accelerated and optimized through conscious effort and practice. This implies that individuals can actively engage with their intuitive faculties, adopting strategies and habits that facilitate the refinement and utilization of intuition in everyday life. By committing regularly to a certain type of practice, such as meditation or reflective journaling, individuals can heighten their awareness of intuitive signals and enhance their ability to discern meaningful insights amid the noise of daily existence.

Additionally, deliberate exposure to novel experiences, diverse perspectives, and challenging situations can stimulate intuitive growth by broadening one's repertoire of mental models and heuristics. Through consistent practice and intentional cultivation, individuals can sharpen their intuition as a valuable tool for decision-making, problem-solving, and personal transformation.

The role of conscious effort and practice underscores the proactive nature of intuition development, highlighting the importance of dedication, perseverance, and discipline in harnessing the full potential of intuitive abilities.

Work with Direct Intuition

What Is Direct Intuition?

Direct intuition is a profound aspect of human cognition as it encompasses immediate insights or gut feelings that emerge spontaneously, guiding decision-making without conscious reasoning. These intuitive impressions, deeply rooted in our subconscious, often arise swiftly and decisively in response to specific situations or dilemmas. Unlike analytical thinking, which relies on logical deduction and systematic evaluation, direct intuition operates on a more intuitive and visceral level, drawing upon emotional cues, past experiences, and implicit knowledge to inform rapid judgments.

By acknowledging these intuitive impulses, individuals can tap into a profound source of guidance and wisdom that transcends conventional modes of rationality. Direct intuition offers a unique lens through which individuals can navigate complex decisions and dilemmas with clarity, confidence, and authenticity, leading to more meaningful and fulfilling outcomes.

Developing this intuitive skill requires cultivating self-awareness, trust, and a willingness to listen to one's inner guidance. It is a journey of exploration and self-discovery, where individuals learn to harness the power of their intuition to navigate life's complexities with grace and insight.

Examples of Direct Intuition

Direct intuitive experiences are diverse in their manifestations and offer valuable insights and guidance across various domains of human experience. Consider a sudden hunch or gut feeling warning a person to avoid a certain situation, prompting them to trust their instincts and take precautionary measures. In high-pressure moments, athletes often rely on intuitive leaps to make split-second decisions with confidence and precision, leading to peak performance. Similarly, creative individuals may experience intuitive flashes of inspiration that guide their artistic process, fueling innovation and breakthroughs.

These examples underscore the versatility and relevance of direct intuition in guiding decision-making, problem-solving, and creativity. By recognizing these intuitive experiences, individuals can harness their innate wisdom to navigate life's challenges more effectively. Whether in mundane daily decisions or pivotal life choices, direct intuition serves as a trusted compass, guiding individuals toward authenticity and fulfillment. Cultivating a deeper awareness of these intuitive signals empowers individuals to embrace their inner wisdom and live in alignment with their true selves.

How to Recognize Direct Intuition?

Recognizing direct intuition necessitates cultivating a heightened sense of self-awareness and attunement to subtle internal signals. Mindfulness practices offer invaluable tools to quiet the noise of the mind and tune into intuitive sensations. Paying attention to bodily sensations, such as tension or relaxation, can provide valuable clues about the presence of intuitive insights. Additionally, maintaining a journal to record intuitive impressions and reflecting on past experiences can enhance one's ability to discern recurring patterns and themes indicative of intuitive guidance.

By creating space for quiet contemplation and introspection, you can sharpen your intuitive awareness and discernment, which will help you to navigate life's challenges and opportunities more effectively. Trusting and acting upon these intuitive signals can lead to greater confidence and alignment with one's authentic path, fostering a deeper connection with one's inner wisdom and guiding principles.

Strengthen Your Direct Intuitive Abilities

Strengthening direct intuitive abilities entails engaging in exercises and activities designed to stimulate intuitive perception and receptivity. Visualization exercises, where individuals immerse themselves in different scenarios and attend to their intuitive responses, can enhance intuitive clarity and vividness. Role-playing exercises, where individuals enact various roles or scenarios and trust their gut instincts to guide their actions, can cultivate confidence in intuitive decision-making. Additionally, practicing intuitive listening—attuning to subtle cues and nonverbal signals in interpersonal interactions—can refine intuitive sensitivity and interpersonal intuition.

By incorporating these exercises into your daily routine, you can cultivate a more intuitive mindset and develop a deeper trust in your innate wisdom and guidance. Consistent practice and reflection allow individuals to refine their intuitive abilities over time, leading to greater clarity, resilience, and authenticity in their life journey.

Work with Indirect Intuition

What Is Indirect Intuition?

Indirect intuition is a complex cognitive process and involves subconscious mechanisms that gradually lead to insights or solutions over time. Unlike direct intuition, which offers immediate clarity, indirect intuition operates subtly beneath conscious awareness, allowing for the integration of various inputs and perspectives. This process often unfolds through a series of subtle nudges, dreams, or reflections, gradually guiding individuals toward understanding without the need for conscious effort.

Indirect intuition invites individuals to embrace uncertainty and trust in the organic unfolding of insights, recognizing that answers may reveal themselves over time. By cultivating patience and openness to the subtle signals of intuition, individuals can tap into a deeper reservoir of wisdom and understanding. Fostering a sense of curiosity and receptivity toward the unknown can enhance the receptiveness to indirect intuitive insights. When uncertainty is embraced as a natural part of the intuitive process, it allows individuals to navigate complexity with greater ease and confidence, leading to profound personal growth and transformation.

Manifestation of Indirect Intuitive Signals

Indirect intuitive signals manifest through a myriad of channels, offering rich insights and revelations. Dreams, often regarded as the language of the subconscious mind, provide symbolic representations of underlying thoughts, emotions, and desires. These nocturnal journeys offer glimpses into the inner landscape of the psyche, illuminating hidden truths and unresolved conflicts. Sudden realizations, colloquially known as "aha" moments, occur when the subconscious mind connects seemingly unrelated pieces of information, resulting in a sudden and profound understanding. Creative breakthroughs, fueled by the subconscious mind's capacity for synthesis and innovation, lead to novel ideas and solutions. These diverse manifestations of indirect intuition highlight its multifaceted nature, showcasing its ability to inspire and inform individuals' lives in profound ways.

Access Indirect Intuitive Cues

Accessing and interpreting indirect intuitive cues requires employing specific techniques and approaches that facilitate subconscious processing. Brainstorming, a creative technique for generating a multitude of ideas rapidly, encourages the free flow of thoughts and associations, tapping into subconscious creativity. Mind mapping provides a visual framework for organizing and exploring interconnected concepts, fostering intuitive insights and connections. Free writing, a process of uninhibited expression, allows individuals to explore subconscious thoughts and emotions, uncovering hidden patterns and associations. Additionally, engaging in activities such as walking in nature, engaging in artistic pursuits, or practicing mindfulness can quiet the conscious mind and create space for subconscious insights to emerge. These techniques serve as gateways to accessing and harnessing the power of indirect intuition, unlocking deeper layers of understanding and creativity.

Improve Indirect Intuitive Insights

Fostering indirect intuitive insights involves embracing practices that promote relaxation, exposure to diverse stimuli, and the incubation of ideas. Engaging in relaxation techniques such as meditation, deep breathing exercises, or progressive muscle relaxation creates a conducive environment for subconscious processing by calming the mind and reducing stress. Exposure to diverse stimuli, whether through reading, attending cultural events, or traveling, stimulates the subconscious mind and encourages new connections and insights. Incubation, the process of allowing ideas to gestate in the subconscious mind over time, provides space for deeper processing and integration, leading to fresh perspectives and innovative solutions. Maintaining a dream journal, practicing active imagination, or engaging in creative activities can also stimulate indirect intuitive insights. By incorporating these practices into daily life, individuals can cultivate and nurture their indirect intuitive abilities, unlocking new levels of creativity, insight, and personal growth.

Integrate Intuition into Decision-Making

A Balanced Approach to Decision-Making

Adopting a balanced approach to decision-making entails gathering relevant information, consulting intuition, and assessing potential outcomes before making decisions. This process involves engaging in thorough research, analysis, and evaluation to gather pertinent data and insights. Additionally, individuals must listen to their intuitive instincts, paying attention to gut feelings, intuitive flashes, and emotional responses that may arise during the decision-making process. After gathering information and consulting intuition, individuals must weigh the potential outcomes and consequences of their decisions, considering both short-term and long-term implications. By integrating analytical reasoning with intuitive guidance, individuals can make more informed and holistic decisions that align with their values, goals, and priorities. This balanced approach allows individuals to leverage the strengths of both rationality and intuition, leading to more confident and effective decision-making outcomes.

Trust and Act upon Intuitive Guidance

Trusting and acting upon intuitive guidance requires cultivating self-awareness, discernment, and confidence in one's intuitive capabilities. This involves developing a deep understanding of one's own intuitive signals and recognizing the subtle cues and patterns that signify intuitive insights. Building trust in intuition requires tuning into inner wisdom, listening to the quiet voice of intuition amid the noise of external influences and expectations. Moreover, individuals must cultivate the courage to follow their intuitive guidance, even when it may contradict rational analysis or conventional wisdom. Trusting intuition involves embracing uncertainty and vulnerability, surrendering to the wisdom of the subconscious mind and the greater universe. By developing confidence in their intuitive capabilities, individuals can navigate life's challenges with greater clarity, resilience, and authenticity, leading to more fulfilling and purposeful experiences. Ultimately, trusting and acting upon intuitive guidance empowers individuals to lead lives that are aligned with their deepest values, desires, and aspirations.

Overcome Challenges and Skepticism

Address Common Challenges and Doubts

When one decides to embrace intuition, they are likely to confront individuals with multifaceted challenges and doubts. Among these challenges, the fear of making mistakes looms large. Many individuals hesitate to trust their intuitive insights, fearing that they may lead to undesirable outcomes or failure. Moreover, societal pressures often prioritize rationality over intuition, leading individuals to doubt the validity and reliability of their intuitive guidance.

Additionally, skepticism, either from within oneself or from external sources, can cast doubt on the credibility of intuitive insights. Past experiences of intuition being dismissed or invalidated can further erode confidence in one's intuitive abilities. Moreover, distinguishing between true intuition and other cognitive biases or emotional responses can present a significant challenge.

Overcoming these obstacles necessitates a comprehensive approach that addresses both internal and external factors. Cultivating self-awareness, discernment, and trust in one's intuitive capabilities forms the foundation for navigating these challenges. When individuals actively address these common doubts and concerns, they can begin to cultivate a more open and receptive mindset toward intuition, paving the way for its transformative potential to unfold.

Strategies for Overcoming Skepticism and Resistance

Overcoming skepticism and resistance to intuitive thinking demands a strategic and holistic approach. Educating oneself about the science and psychology behind intuition is a crucial first step. Understanding the evolutionary roots of intuition and its role in human decision-making can help dispel misconceptions and foster a deeper appreciation for its value. Engaging in personal reflection and introspection can provide opportunities to connect with one's intuitive insights on a deeper level. Seeking out supportive communities and mentors who value and encourage intuitive thinking can offer validation and encouragement along the intuitive journey.

Additionally, actively challenging and reframing skeptical beliefs and attitudes toward intuition is essential. This involves examining the evidence and experiences that support the validity of intuitive insights, as well as cultivating a mindset of curiosity and openness toward intuitive guidance. By adopting these strategies, individuals can gradually overcome skepticism and resistance, and pave the way for a more harmonious integration of intuition into their life.

Real-Life Examples

Imagine a moment when your intuition guided you through a difficult decision or led you to an unexpected opportunity. These transformative experiences are more common than you might think. These stories offer tangible examples of how intuition can positively influence decision-making, personal development, and life experiences. By delving into these narratives, you'll gain insight into how intuition operates in various contexts, providing inspiration and validation for your own intuitive experiences. Whether it's a career choice, a relationship decision, or a moment of creative inspiration, these stories illustrate the universal nature of intuition and its power to guide and support us on our unique paths.

Conclusion

In this chapter, we began with the recognition that intuition is not an exclusive gift bestowed upon a select few but a skill that can be developed through conscious effort and practice. Drawing upon research and real-life examples, we uncovered the transformative potential of intuition as a guiding force in decision-making, problem-solving, and personal transformation.

Direct intuition emerged as a profound aspect of human cognition, offering immediate insights that transcend conscious reasoning. From gut feelings to intuitive flashes of inspiration, we learned to trust and embrace these intuitive impulses as valuable sources of wisdom and guidance.

Indirect intuition, on the other hand, operates subtly beneath conscious awareness, gradually leading to insights and solutions over time. By cultivating patience, openness, and receptivity to the subtle signals of intuition, we discovered the power of embracing uncertainty and trusting in the organic unfolding of insights.

Integration of intuition into decision-making emerged as a balanced approach that combines analytical reasoning with intuitive guidance. By gathering relevant information, consulting intuition, and assessing potential outcomes, individuals can make informed and holistic decisions that align with their values and goals.

Yet our journey was not without its challenges and doubts. Fear of making mistakes, societal pressures, and skepticism often cast shadows on the path of intuition. However, through education, reflection, and community support, we learned to overcome these obstacles and cultivate a more open and receptive mindset toward intuition.

Real-life examples served as beacons of inspiration, illuminating the transformative power of intuition in guiding us through difficult decisions, unexpected opportunities, and moments of creative inspiration.

As we conclude this chapter, let us embrace intuition not as a mysterious force but as a profound aspect of our humanity—a skill to be honed, a wisdom to be trusted, and a guiding light on our journey toward authenticity and fulfillment.

Chapter Six

Eliminate Bad Habits

Here, we confront the barriers that hinder our intuitive clarity and explore the transformative journey of eliminating bad habits to unleash our intuitive potential.

In this chapter, we delve into the insidious impact of detrimental habits on our intuition. From the automatic responses that cloud our judgment to the influence of cognitive biases on our perception, we uncover the ways in which these habits obstruct our ability to tap into our inner wisdom.

But it's not just our internal landscape that shapes our intuitive experiences; external factors play a crucial role as well. We examine the environments that either nurture or inhibit intuition, providing insights into the importance of selecting spaces conducive to intuitive clarity.

Furthermore, we confront the modern-day epidemic of multitasking, which fragments our attention and diminishes our capacity for deep intuitive insight. By breaking free from the multitasking trap and prioritizing tasks with intentionality, we create space for heightened focus and intuitive awareness.

Yet nurturing our intuition goes beyond mere environmental and behavioral adjustments; it necessitates a holistic approach that prioritizes mental well-being. We explore the symbiotic relationship between mental health and intuitive abilities, offering practical strategies for managing challenges and incorporating self-care into our daily routines.

This chapter serves as a call to action—a call to shed the shackles of bad habits and cultivate an environment that fosters intuitive clarity and growth.

Impact of Bad Habits on Intuition

Automatic Responses

Bad habits often operate on autopilot, bypassing our conscious decision-making processes. This automaticity diminishes our ability to pause, reflect, and tune into our intuition before acting. Instead, we react impulsively, driven by ingrained patterns of behavior that may not align with our true desires or values.

Automatic responses can be triggered by various factors, such as environmental cues, emotional states, or social influences. For example, reaching for a cigarette when feeling stressed or checking social media compulsively when bored are common automatic responses driven by habit.

To overcome automatic responses and enhance intuition, it's essential to cultivate mindfulness and self-awareness. By consciously observing our thoughts, emotions, and behaviors, we can interrupt the automatic cycle and create space for more intentional decision-making. Techniques like mindfulness meditation, deep breathing exercises, or journaling can help us become more attuned to our inner workings and break free from the grip of automatic habits. Through consistent practice and self-reflection, we can gradually rewire our brain's neural pathways, replacing automatic responses with more conscious and intuitive actions.

Distorted Perception

Habitual behaviors can distort our perception of reality, leading us to overlook important cues or signals that could inform intuitive decision-making. For example, someone with a habit of negative thinking may interpret neutral situations as threats, clouding their judgment and intuition.

Distorted perception can stem from deep-seated beliefs, past experiences, or societal conditioning. These biases color our interpretation of events, shaping our understanding of the world around us. In the context of intuition, distorted perception can prevent us from accurately assessing situations and making informed choices.

To counteract distorted perception and enhance intuition, it's crucial to cultivate a mindset of curiosity and open-mindedness. By challenging our assumptions and examining situations from multiple perspectives, we can overcome cognitive biases and see beyond our habitual ways of thinking. Practices like cognitive reframing, empathy-building exercises, and exposure to diverse viewpoints can help broaden our outlook and sharpen our intuitive faculties.

The Relationship between Self-Control and Intuition

Self-control plays a crucial role in shaping our habits and, consequently, our intuitive abilities. A lack of self-control often leads to impulsive decision-making, where we prioritize short-term gratification over long-term goals. By cultivating self-control, we empower ourselves to pause, reflect, and tap into our intuition more effectively.

The relationship between self-control and intuition is bidirectional, with each influencing the other in a dynamic interplay. When we exercise self-control, we strengthen our ability to resist temptations and make thoughtful choices aligned with our values and goals. This, in turn, enhances our intuitive capacities by allowing us to access deeper insights and inner wisdom.

To cultivate self-control and enhance intuition, it's essential to practice self-discipline and self-regulation. Setting clear goals, establishing routines, and developing strategies for managing impulses can help strengthen our self-control muscle over time. Additionally, techniques like mindfulness meditation, cognitive behavioral therapy, and stress management can support us in navigating challenges and making wise decisions in alignment with our intuition.

The Psychology of Cognitive Biases

Influence of Cognitive Biases on Intuition

Cognitive biases are mental shortcuts that our brains use to process information efficiently. While they can be useful in simplifying complex situations, they often lead to errors in judgment. In the context of intuition, cognitive biases can cloud our perception of reality and hinder our ability to make accurate assessments. For example, confirmation bias causes us to seek out information that confirms our existing beliefs while ignoring contradictory evidence. This bias can prevent us from considering alternative viewpoints and lead to narrow-minded decision-making. Similarly, the availability heuristic causes us to overestimate the likelihood of events based on how easily they come to mind, leading to skewed judgments. By understanding these biases, we can become more aware of their influence on our intuition and take steps to mitigate their effects.

Examples of Common Biases

Confirmation bias, one of the most prevalent biases, occurs when we selectively seek out information that confirms our preconceptions while disregarding contradictory evidence. For instance, a manager may favor hiring candidates who validate their initial impressions during interviews, overlooking red flags that suggest otherwise. Availability heuristic refers to our tendency to overestimate the likelihood of events based on how readily examples come to mind. For example, individuals may perceive flying as riskier than driving because plane crashes receive more media coverage despite statistical evidence suggesting otherwise.

Anchoring bias occurs when we rely too heavily on the first piece of information we encounter when making decisions. For instance, negotiators may be influenced by initial offers, anchoring their subsequent counteroffers closer to the initial figure. These examples illustrate how cognitive biases can distort our intuitive thinking and lead to suboptimal decision-making outcomes.

Danger of Biases

Biases can distort intuitive thinking by leading us to make judgments based on flawed reasoning rather than objective reality. They create blind spots in our perception, making it challenging to see situations accurately. As a result, our intuitive judgments may be skewed, leading to poor decision-making outcomes. It's essential to approach intuitive thinking with caution and skepticism, recognizing the potential influence of biases.

By questioning our assumptions, seeking out diverse perspectives, and actively challenging our cognitive tendencies, we can mitigate the impact of biases on our intuition. Additionally, fostering a culture of open-mindedness and critical thinking within teams and organizations can help counteract the detrimental effects of biases on collective decision-making processes. So, by acknowledging the presence of biases and adopting strategies to counteract them, we can enhance the accuracy and effectiveness of our intuitive judgments.

Choose Environments Conducive to Intuition

Importance of Environmental Factors

The significance of environmental factors in nurturing intuition cannot be overstated. Our surroundings wield a profound influence on our psychological and emotional well-being, directly impacting the clarity and strength of our intuitive faculties. Environments characterized by tranquility, such as serene natural landscapes or serene meditation spaces, offer fertile ground for intuitive insights to emerge. These settings, devoid of external disturbances, enable us to delve deeply into introspection, fostering a profound connection with our intuition. Research from 2022 published in *Frontiers of Psychiatry* underscores the transformative effects of natural environments on cognitive functioning and creativity, highlighting their ability to amplify intuitive decision-making.

What Environments Should You Target?

Deliberately seeking out environments conducive to learning and self-awareness is pivotal in honing and amplifying our intuitive abilities. Environments that foster curiosity, exploration, and self-reflection serve as fertile grounds for intuitive growth. Whether it's the quiet ambiance of a library, the inspiring atmosphere of an art gallery, or the tranquil setting of a meditation retreat, these spaces provide respite from external distractions, allowing us to embark on a journey of self-discovery.

Moreover, surrounding yourselves with individuals who stimulate and challenge your intellect cultivates a deeper level of self-awareness and enhances our intuitive capacities. When intentionally immerse ourselves in environments that stimulate growth and self-reflection, you expand our understanding of ourselves and the world around us, thereby enriching our intuitive decision-making prowess.

Strategies for Avoiding Certain Environments

In today's fast-paced and digitally saturated world, navigating distractions poses a formidable challenge to maintaining focus and clarity essential for intuitive decision-making. To optimize our intuitive abilities, it is imperative to identify and mitigate factors that undermine concentration and cognitive functioning. This necessitates implementing a repertoire of strategies aimed at cultivating environments conducive to intuition. Establishing firm boundaries around technology use, carving out designated workspaces devoid of clutter and noise, and incorporating regular breaks for mental rejuvenation are potent tactics for minimizing distractions and enhancing focus. By proactively curating their environment and nurturing habits that prioritize mental clarity, individuals create an optimal milieu for intuition to flourish, empowering us to make discerning and enlightened decisions across all domains of life.

Breaking the Multitasking Trap

The Negative Effects of Multitasking

Multitasking, once hailed as a productivity hack, has been increasingly recognized for its detrimental impact on cognitive function and intuition. The allure of juggling multiple tasks simultaneously can lead to a false sense of efficiency, but research underscores its toll on mental performance. When we engage in multitasking, our brains are forced to rapidly switch between tasks, expending valuable cognitive resources in the process. This constant task-switching taxes our working memory, impairs our ability to retain information, and leads to a decline in overall productivity.

Furthermore, multitasking inhibits deep processing and reflection, both essential components of intuitive decision-making. Our intuition thrives when we can focus our attention fully on a single task, allowing us to tap into our subconscious wisdom and make insightful judgments. However, the fragmented attention demanded by multitasking disrupts this process, leaving us with muddled intuition and compromised decision-making abilities.

When individuals recognize the negative effects of multitasking on cognitive function and intuition, they can take proactive steps to mitigate its impact. Instead of succumbing to the allure of multitasking, they can prioritize tasks based on importance and allocate dedicated time blocks to focus on each task individually. This intentional approach allows them to preserve cognitive resources, maintain focus, and tap into their intuition more effectively.

Tips for Prioritizing Tasks

Prioritizing tasks and focusing attention on one thing at a time is essential for optimizing cognitive function and intuition. Rather than succumbing to the pressure to multitask, we can employ strategies to streamline our workflow and enhance our ability to concentrate fully on each task. Begin by identifying the most critical tasks on the to-do list and allocating dedicated time blocks to focus on each task individually. Setting clear goals and deadlines helps maintain accountability and ensures progress toward completion.

In addition to task prioritization, the practice of single-tasking can be a game-changer for enhancing cognitive function and intuition. Single-tasking involves dedicating your full attention and energy to one task until completion before moving on to the next. This focused approach allows for deeper engagement with the task at hand, fostering greater clarity of thought and more insightful decision-making.

Productivity techniques such as the Pomodoro Technique can further enhance concentration and productivity by breaking work into focused intervals followed by short breaks. By alternating periods of intense focus with brief moments of rest, you can maintain mental freshness and sustain peak performance throughout the day.

Techniques for Improving Mental Clarity and Concentration

Improving mental clarity and concentration is essential for overcoming the multitasking trap and harnessing the power of intuition. Incorporate mindfulness practices into your daily routine to cultivate a heightened sense of presence and focus. Take regular breaks throughout the day to rest and recharge your mental faculties, allowing your mind to reset and rejuvenate.

Additionally, optimize your physical environment by minimizing distractions and creating a dedicated workspace conducive to concentration. Stay organized and declutter your surroundings to promote mental clarity and reduce cognitive load.

Finally, prioritize self-care activities such as adequate sleep, exercise, and nutrition to support overall brain health and cognitive function. By implementing these techniques for improving mental clarity and concentration, you can break free from the multitasking trap and unlock your full intuitive potential.

Prioritize Mental Health for Enhanced Intuition

Link between Mental Well-Being and Intuitive Abilities

The link between mental well-being and intuitive abilities is intricate and profound. When we are mentally balanced and emotionally centered, our intuition operates at its peak, guiding us with clarity and insight. Conversely, stress, anxiety, and other mental health challenges can cloud our intuitive faculties, hindering our ability to access inner wisdom and make discerning decisions. Research has shown that individuals with higher levels of psychological well-being demonstrate greater intuition and cognitive flexibility, underscoring the importance of mental wellness in nurturing intuitive capabilities. By prioritizing mental health, we not only foster a greater sense of inner peace and fulfillment but also unleash the full power of our intuition to navigate life's complexities with confidence and clarity.

Practical Steps for Managing Mental Health Challenges

Managing stress, anxiety, and other mental health challenges is essential for optimizing intuition and overall well-being. Begin by identifying sources of stress and implementing strategies to mitigate their impact. This may involve practicing relaxation techniques such as deep breathing exercises, progressive muscle relaxation, or mindfulness meditation to induce a state of calm and relaxation. Engaging in regular physical activity, maintaining a balanced diet, and prioritizing adequate sleep are also crucial for managing stress and promoting mental resilience.

Additionally, cultivating healthy coping mechanisms and seeking support from friends, family, or mental health professionals can provide valuable resources for navigating challenging emotions and experiences. Cognitive behavioral techniques such as cognitive restructuring and reframing can help challenge negative thought patterns and promote a more positive outlook on life.

By taking proactive steps to manage stress, anxiety, and other mental health challenges, we create space for intuition to thrive, enabling us to make more insightful and intuitive decisions in all aspects of our lives.

Incorporate Self-Care Routines into Daily Life

Establishing a consistent self-care routine that encompasses physical, emotional, and spiritual well-being is key to maintaining mental equilibrium and supporting intuitive development. By dedicating time each day to nourish our minds, bodies, and spirits, we foster a deeper connection with ourselves and cultivate the inner resources necessary for intuitive insight and discernment. Ultimately, by prioritizing mental health and integrating mindfulness practices and self-care routines into our daily lives, we lay the groundwork for enhanced intuition and overall well-being.

Develop Positive Habits

Get Rid of Bad Habits

Replacing bad habits with positive ones is a transformative process that requires self-awareness, intentionality, and perseverance. Begin by identifying the habits that detract from intuitive living, whether it's excessive screen time, unhealthy eating patterns, or negative self-talk. Once identified, consciously choose to replace these habits with positive alternatives that align with your values and goals. For example, if you find yourself reaching for unhealthy snacks when stressed, replace this habit with a healthier coping mechanism, such as going for a walk or practicing mindfulness. By consistently reinforcing positive behaviors, you gradually rewire your brain's neural pathways, making intuitive living more accessible and sustainable.

Cultivate Positive Habits

Cultivating habits, such as journaling, meditation, and reflection, is instrumental in promoting intuition and self-awareness. Journaling allows us to externalize our thoughts and emotions, providing clarity and insight into our inner world. Set aside time each day to write freely, exploring your thoughts, feelings, and experiences without judgment. Meditation cultivates present-moment awareness and inner calm, allowing us to quiet the noise of the mind and connect with our intuitive guidance. Incorporate a daily meditation practice into your routine, even if it's just a few minutes of focused breathing or mindfulness.

Reflection involves introspection and evaluation of past experiences, allowing us to glean valuable lessons and insights. Set aside time regularly to reflect on your actions, decisions, and the impact they've had on your life.

Conclusion

We've explored how detrimental habits, whether they be automatic responses, distorted perceptions, or the modern-day trap of multitasking, obstruct our intuitive clarity. We've recognized the vital role of environments conducive to intuition, emphasizing the importance of curating spaces that foster focus and introspection. Moreover, we've delved into the symbiotic relationship between self-control and intuition, understanding how cultivating discipline empowers us to make mindful choices aligned with our intuitive guidance.

Understanding the psychology of cognitive biases has shed light on the pitfalls of flawed reasoning, urging us to challenge our assumptions and broaden our perspectives. We've acknowledged the significance of prioritizing mental health, recognizing that a balanced mind is essential for accessing our inner wisdom. By incorporating self-care routines into our daily lives and replacing negative habits with positive ones, we pave the way for intuitive living.

As we conclude this chapter on eliminating bad habits to unleash our intuitive potential, let us commit to shedding the shackles of bad habits and embracing a lifestyle that nurtures intuitive clarity and insight. Create accountability by sharing your goals with a trusted friend or mentor who can offer support and encouragement along the way. Remember that habits take time to develop, so be patient with yourself and stay committed to your growth journey. By prioritizing consistency and perseverance, you lay the foundation for intuitive living, empowering yourself to live a life aligned with your highest aspirations and deepest truths.

Chapter Seven

Practice and Improve

In this chapter, we continue on our journey of growth and refinement as we explore the art of practicing and improving our intuitive abilities. We need to recognize that intuition, like any skill, thrives with practice and dedication. We understand that the subtle nuances of social cues and interactions play a crucial role in honing our intuition, guiding us toward deeper insights and understanding.

As we navigate the complexities of human interaction, we embrace the importance of structured routines and deliberate practice. We acknowledge that growth requires consistency and commitment, and we let go of the fear of imperfection, understanding that mistakes are an integral part of the learning process.

Through seeking feedback and leveraging available resources, we empower ourselves to continuously evolve and refine our intuitive skills. We embrace technology as a tool for growth and celebrate our achievements and milestones along the way.

The Power of Social Cues

Importance of Social Cues in Intuitive Processing

Understanding the significance of social cues is paramount in the development and refinement of intuitive abilities. Social cues encompass a vast array of signals, both verbal and nonverbal, that convey invaluable information about the thoughts, feelings, and intentions of others. These cues serve as subtle yet potent indicators that can inform our intuitive judgments and guide our interactions with others. By attuning yourself to these cues, you gain deeper insights into the underlying dynamics of social situations, which allows you to navigate them with greater sensitivity and finesse.

Moreover, social cues provide vital clues about the authenticity and trustworthiness of individuals, enabling us to discern genuine connections from superficial ones. Recognizing the importance of social cues lays the groundwork for honing your intuitive processing skills, and empowers you to make more informed and effective decisions in various interpersonal contexts.

Importance of Body Language

Body language and nonverbal cues constitute a rich tapestry of communication that often speaks volumes beyond words alone. From facial expressions and gestures to posture and tone of voice, these subtle cues convey a wealth of information about a person's emotions, intentions, and attitudes. By paying attention to these nonverbal signals, we gain access to a deeper layer of understanding that complements and enriches our intuitive processing.

For example, crossed arms may indicate defensiveness or discomfort, while a genuine smile can signify warmth and openness. Mastering the art of deciphering body language allows us to access a treasure trove of insights that might otherwise remain hidden, empowering us to navigate social interactions with heightened awareness and discernment. Basically, the ability to interpret body language and nonverbal cues is a valuable skill that enhances our intuitive acumen and fosters more meaningful connections with others.

Interpret Social Cues Effectively

The ability to interpret social cues effectively confers numerous benefits across a spectrum of interpersonal scenarios. In professional settings, adeptness at reading nonverbal cues can facilitate successful negotiations, enhance leadership capabilities, and foster cohesive teamwork. By discerning subtle shifts in body language and vocal tone, individuals can gauge the receptiveness of their audience and tailor their communication strategies accordingly. Similarly, in personal relationships, the skill of interpreting social cues fosters deeper empathy, fosters stronger rapport, and cultivates trust and mutual understanding. Furthermore, in unfamiliar or potentially risky situations, the ability to accurately assess social cues can serve as a protective mechanism, helping individuals navigate potential threats and make informed decisions about their safety and well-being.

Practice Intuition through Structured Routines

Importance of Active Practice

Understanding the vital role of active practice is fundamental to nurturing intuition. Active practice involves engaging deliberately in exercises designed to sharpen intuitive skills. It's not merely about passively absorbing information but actively participating in activities that challenge and stimulate intuitive faculties. Recognizing the importance of active practice instills a proactive mindset, driving individuals to seek out opportunities to hone their intuition continuously. By acknowledging that intuition, like any other skill, requires consistent effort and dedication, individuals are empowered to take ownership of their intuitive development journey. Embracing active practice also fosters a sense of agency, allowing individuals to proactively shape their intuitive abilities rather than passively waiting for them to improve. Understanding the importance of active practice lays the foundation for a proactive and empowered approach to developing intuition.

Improve Intuition in Everyday Interactions

Everyday interactions and decision-making processes present abundant opportunities for refining intuition. Employing a diverse range of techniques amplifies intuitive perception and fosters a deeper understanding of situations. Strategies such as empathetic observation, sensory awareness, and pattern recognition serve as powerful tools for honing intuitive abilities.

Empathetic observation entails not only listening actively but also empathizing with others' perspectives, allowing for a more comprehensive understanding of their thoughts and emotions. Sensory awareness practices cultivate mindfulness of both internal and external stimuli, heightening sensitivity to subtle cues and facilitating intuitive decision-making. Meanwhile, pattern recognition involves identifying recurring themes or behaviors in various contexts, enabling individuals to anticipate outcomes and make informed choices based on intuitive insights.

Moreover, engaging in immersive experiences and role-playing exercises provides opportunities to simulate real-life scenarios, refining intuitive responses and enhancing adaptability. By integrating these diverse techniques into daily interactions and decision-making processes, individuals can systematically strengthen their intuitive capabilities, enhancing their ability to navigate complexities and make impactful decisions with confidence and clarity.

Create a Structured Practice Routine

Establishing a structured practice routine is essential for consistent improvement in intuition. Designating specific times and activities dedicated to intuition practice ensures regular engagement and progress. Whether you engage in journaling, role-playing, or meditation, a structured routine provides a framework for deliberate practice and skill development. Consistency breeds familiarity and mastery, as individuals immerse themselves in intentional exercises tailored to strengthen intuitive abilities.

By prioritizing and scheduling practice sessions, individuals demonstrate commitment to their personal growth and development, laying the groundwork for long-term success. A structured practice routine also instills discipline and accountability, preventing procrastination and ensuring that intuitive practice remains a priority amid life's myriad distractions.

Additionally, by establishing a routine, individuals can create a conducive environment for focused learning and improvement, maximizing the effectiveness of their practice sessions. Creating a structured practice routine gives them a sense of purpose and direction and empowers them to make tangible progress in improving their intuitive skills and realizing their full potential.

Set Realistic Goals and Milestones

Setting realistic goals and milestones within the practice routine provides direction and motivation for intuitive development. Goals should be specific, measurable, achievable, relevant, and time-bound (SMART), ensuring clarity and accountability. Breaking down larger objectives into smaller, manageable tasks allows for incremental progress and celebrates achievements along the way. By setting realistic expectations, individuals avoid feelings of overwhelm or inadequacy, fostering a positive mindset conducive to continued growth and improvement.

Also, setting goals within the practice routine provides a roadmap for intuitive development, guiding individuals on their journey toward mastery. By establishing clear benchmarks and milestones, one can track their progress and adjust their approach as needed to stay on course. Celebrating small victories along the way boosts morale and reinforces the belief that progress is attainable with persistence and effort.

Integrate Intuition Practice into Daily Life

Integrating intuition practice into daily life is crucial for sustained growth and development. By incorporating intuitive exercises seamlessly into routines and decision-making processes, individuals reinforce their commitment to personal growth. Consistent integration fosters a deepened understanding and appreciation of intuitive cues and empowers them to make more informed and intuitive decisions in all aspects of life.

Furthermore, integrating intuition practice into daily life promotes consistency and habit formation, ensuring that intuitive development remains a priority amid life's demands and distractions. By making intuition practice a natural and integral part of daily routines, one creates a conducive environment for continuous growth and improvement.

Over time, this holistic approach to intuitive development cultivates a heightened sense of self-awareness and intuition, enhancing overall well-being and effectiveness in various spheres of life.

Consistency and Commitment to Regular Practice

Consistency and commitment to regular practice are paramount for improving intuitive skills over time. Intuition, like any other skill, requires dedicated effort and repetition to develop and strengthen. By prioritizing consistent practice sessions and maintaining unwavering commitment to personal growth, individuals lay the groundwork for lasting improvement.

Emphasizing the importance of consistency instills discipline and resilience and enables individuals to persevere through challenges and setbacks along their intuitive development journey. Over time, the cumulative effects of consistent practice manifest in heightened intuition, improved decision-making abilities, and enhanced overall well-being.

Additionally, regular practice fosters a sense of familiarity and comfort with intuitive processes, making them more readily accessible in various situations. Through consistent and committed practice, individuals cultivate a deep sense of trust in their intuition, allowing them to navigate life's complexities with confidence and clarity.

Overcome the Fear of Imperfection

The Detrimental Effects of Perfectionism

Perfectionism can act as a significant barrier to the development and utilization of intuition. The relentless pursuit of flawlessness often leads individuals to second-guess their intuitive instincts, fearing that any decision made will fall short of an unattainable standard. This perfectionist mindset stifles intuition by promoting hesitation, self-doubt, and over-analysis, preventing individuals from trusting their gut feelings and embracing uncertainty.

Perfectionism provokes a fear of failure, causing individuals to avoid taking risks or making decisions altogether, further impeding intuitive development. By exploring the detrimental effects of perfectionism on intuition, individuals can gain insight into the underlying beliefs and behaviors that hinder their intuitive abilities. Recognizing perfectionism as a limiting factor allows them to challenge and overcome these ingrained patterns and allows a more open and receptive mindset toward intuitive thinking.

By letting go of the need for perfection, one can free oneself to embrace the spontaneity and creativity inherent in intuitive decision-making, unlocking their full potential for growth and self-discovery.

Embrace Imperfection as a Natural Part of the Learning Process

Embracing imperfection is essential for fostering a healthy relationship with intuition. Recognizing that mistakes and setbacks are an inherent part of the learning process allows you to approach intuition with greater openness and acceptance. It liberates individuals from the pressure to always be right or have all the answers, creating space for exploration, experimentation, and growth. You can cultivate a mindset of curiosity and resilience, viewing failures as valuable learning opportunities rather than insurmountable obstacles.

Accepting imperfection promotes a sense of humility and empathy, as individuals acknowledge their own limitations and recognize the inherent humanity in others. They can develop a more compassionate and forgiving attitude toward themself and others, creating a supportive environment conducive to intuitive development.

Let Go of the Need for Flawless Intuition

Letting go of the need for flawless intuition is essential for unleashing its full potential. Rather than striving for perfection, individuals are encouraged to focus on growth and progress. This shift in mindset allows individuals to approach intuition with greater flexibility and adaptability, embracing the ebb and flow of intuitive insights without judgment or self-criticism. Strategies for letting go of the need for flawless intuition include cultivating self-compassion, practicing mindfulness, and reframing failure as a stepping-stone to success.

By acknowledging and accepting the inevitability of imperfection, individuals can free themselves from the paralyzing grip of perfectionism and tap into the transformative power of intuitive thinking. When they let go of the need for flawless intuition and embrace growth instead, they can unlock their innate potential for creativity, innovation, and self-discovery, leading to greater fulfillment and success in all areas of life.

Cultivating Intuition through Feedback

Importance of Seeking Feedback

Seeking feedback is integral to the development and refinement of intuitive abilities. Feedback provides valuable insights and perspectives that individuals may not have considered on their own. By soliciting feedback from others, they can gain a more comprehensive understanding of their strengths and areas for improvement, and it helps them to fine-tune their intuitive skills effectively.

Feedback also serves as a mirror, reflecting how our actions and decisions are perceived by others and providing invaluable information for self-reflection and growth. Seeking feedback demonstrates humility and a willingness to learn and shows a culture of collaboration and continuous improvement. By actively seeking feedback, individuals demonstrate a commitment to their personal and professional development, positioning themselves for success in various aspects of life. Embracing feedback as a catalyst for growth empowers individuals to harness the full potential of their intuitive abilities, leading to greater self-awareness, effectiveness, and fulfillment.

Solicit Constructive Criticism and Learn from Mistakes

Soliciting constructive criticism and learning from mistakes are essential skills for cultivating intuition. Effective feedback requires creating a safe and supportive environment where individuals feel comfortable sharing their honest opinions and observations. To solicit constructive criticism, one should approach feedback sessions with an open mind and a willingness to listen actively. One should ask specific, open-ended questions that encourage detailed responses and provide context for the feedback being sought.

Individuals should also express gratitude for the feedback received and demonstrate a commitment to taking actionable steps toward improvement. Learning from mistakes involves embracing failure as an opportunity for growth rather than a reflection of personal inadequacy. By adopting a growth mindset, they can extract valuable lessons from their experiences, identify areas for improvement, and implement strategies to enhance their intuitive abilities.

Leveraging Technology and Resources

Explore Apps, Books, Courses, and Other Learning Materials

Exploring apps, books, courses, and other learning materials provides individuals with a wealth of opportunities to deepen their understanding of intuition and develop their intuitive skills. Apps offer convenient and accessible ways to practice mindfulness, track intuitive insights, and access guided meditation sessions. Books provide in-depth knowledge and insights from experts in the field, offering valuable guidance and inspiration for individuals seeking to enhance their intuition. Courses and workshops offer structured learning experiences, allowing individuals to delve deeper into specific aspects of intuition and receive personalized guidance and feedback.

By exploring a diverse range of learning materials, individuals can tailor their learning experience to suit their preferences and learning style, ensuring a more engaging and effective learning journey. Moreover, exploring apps, books, courses, and other learning materials encourages them to stay curious and open-minded and helps them attain a lifelong commitment to learning and personal growth. By embracing a variety of learning resources, one can expand their horizons, deepen their understanding of intuition, and unlock their full potential for personal and professional success.

Here is a list of apps, books, courses, and other learning materials built to help develop intuitive skills:

- Insight Timer: This meditation app offers a variety of guided meditations and courses focused on intuition, mindfulness, and spiritual development.

- Headspace: While primarily a meditation app, Headspace includes content on mindfulness and awareness, which can contribute to developing intuitive abilities.

- Aura: This app provides personalized meditation and mindfulness exercises tailored to individual preferences, supporting users in connecting with their intuition.

- *The Intuitive Way* by Penney Peirce: This book is a guide to developing intuition and understanding the language of energy and the higher self.

- *Intuition: Knowing Beyond Logic* by Osho: A book that provides a philosophical perspective on intuition, exploring its nature and how it can be cultivated.

- *Develop Your Intuition in 5 Easy Steps*: This Udemy course covers practical exercises to unlock and strengthen intuition.

- Hay House (https://www.hayhouse.co.uk): This website offers a range of courses by intuitive and spiritual teachers, covering topics like intuition, energy healing, and spiritual development.

- *The Intuitive Hour* or *Intuitive Insights*: These podcasts help gain insights from experts and practitioners in the field of intuition.

Use Technology to Develop Intuition

Technology can play a significant role in aiding the practice and development of intuition, offering innovative solutions and tools to support individuals in their journey toward intuitive mastery. From wearable devices that track biometric data to AI-powered apps that provide personalized insights and recommendations, technology offers a myriad of possibilities for enhancing intuition skills. For example, biofeedback devices can help individuals tune into their physiological responses, providing valuable feedback on their stress levels and emotional state. Virtual reality simulations can create immersive learning experiences, allowing individuals to practice decision-making in realistic scenarios and receive instant feedback on their intuitive responses.

Technology also enables individuals to connect with like-minded individuals and experts in the field through online communities, webinars, and social media platforms, fostering collaboration and knowledge sharing. By harnessing the power of technology, individuals can leverage cutting-edge tools and resources to accelerate their intuitive development and achieve greater levels of success and fulfillment in all aspects of life.

Track Progress and Celebrate Successes

Importance of Monitoring Progress

Monitoring progress is crucial for individuals on their journey of intuitive development. Tracking improvement over time provides valuable insights into the effectiveness of various practices and techniques employed. It allows individuals to identify patterns, trends, and areas of strength and weakness in their intuitive abilities. Moreover, monitoring progress fosters accountability and motivation, as individuals witness tangible evidence of their growth and improvement. By keeping track of their progress, individuals can set realistic goals, adjust their approach as needed, and stay committed to their intuitive development journey.

Additionally, monitoring progress provides a sense of direction and purpose, guiding individuals toward continuous improvement and success. Whether it's through journaling, keeping a log of intuitive experiences, or using tracking apps, the act of monitoring progress empowers individuals to take ownership of their growth and make informed decisions about their intuitive development. Prioritizing the importance of monitoring progress, individuals can accelerate their growth, achieve their goals, and unlock their full potential for intuitive thinking and decision-making.

Strategies for Measuring and Assessing Intuitive Growth

Developing strategies for measuring and assessing intuitive growth is essential for individuals seeking to enhance their intuitive abilities. Effective measurement allows individuals to quantify their progress and identify areas for improvement accurately. Strategies for measuring intuitive growth may include self-assessment tools, performance metrics, or qualitative evaluations based on feedback from peers or mentors. Additionally, individuals can use benchmarks and milestones to gauge their progress and celebrate achievements along the way. By developing systematic methods for measuring and assessing intuitive growth, individuals can gain valuable insights into their strengths and weaknesses and make informed decisions about their development.

Moreover, measuring and assessing intuitive growth fosters a culture of continuous learning and improvement, as individuals strive to achieve higher levels of proficiency and mastery. By implementing effective strategies for measuring and assessing intuitive growth, individuals can accelerate their development, achieve their goals, and unlock their full potential for intuitive thinking and decision-making.

Celebrate Achievements and Milestones

Celebrating achievements and milestones is essential for individuals on their journey of self-improvement. Recognizing and acknowledging progress boosts morale, motivation, and self-confidence, reinforcing the belief that growth is attainable with persistence and effort. Celebrating achievements also provides an opportunity for reflection and gratitude, allowing individuals to pause and appreciate how far they've come.

Moreover, celebrating milestones develops a sense of community and support, as individuals share their successes with friends, family, or peers who have supported them along the way. By celebrating achievements and milestones, individuals cultivate a positive and empowering mindset. Whether it's through small rewards, social gatherings, or personal reflections, the act of celebrating achievements and milestones encourages people to stay committed to their goals and persevere through challenges.

Ultimately, by prioritizing the importance of celebrating achievements and milestones, individuals develop a culture of positivity, resilience, and growth, which empowers them to thrive in all aspects of life.

Conclusion

In the journey of self-improvement and intuitive development, the path to mastery is paved with dedication, practice, and a commitment to growth. Throughout this chapter, we've explored the foundational principles of developing intuition through structured routines, beginning with small, low-stakes situations, establishing disciplined practice regimens, and seamlessly integrating intuitive thinking into our daily lives.

By starting with small, manageable tasks, we build the confidence needed to tackle more significant challenges, while also cultivating an awareness of the subtle cues guiding our decisions. Through the establishment of structured practice routines, we ensure consistent engagement with our intuition, fostering steady progress and refinement of our intuitive abilities over time. Additionally, by embracing intuition as an integral aspect of our daily routines, we deepen our connection to this innate faculty, empowering ourselves to make more informed, authentic choices in every aspect of our lives.

Always remember that the journey of intuitive development is not linear; it is a continuous process of growth and exploration. Embrace each step of the journey with openness and curiosity, acknowledging that imperfection is not a flaw but rather an opportunity for learning and refinement. Keep practicing, keep evolving, and trust in the wisdom of your intuition to guide you toward greater clarity, purpose, and fulfillment in life.

Chapter Eight
Get Your Sh** Together

In this final chapter, we confront the inevitable challenges and setbacks that arise on the journey of sharpening our intuition, and we explore strategies to navigate them with resilience and grace. We acknowledge the tumultuous nature of life and the hurdles we encounter along the way. From unexpected setbacks to moments of doubt, we confront these obstacles head-on, recognizing them as opportunities for growth and self-discovery.

We understand that prioritizing mental health is paramount to nurturing our intuition. Through mindfulness practices and meditation, we cultivate inner peace and clarity, fostering a deeper connection with ourselves and our intuitive insights.

In moments of uncertainty, we remind ourselves to simply relax—to let go of the need for control and allow intuition to guide us forward. We embrace the support of others, seeking help when needed and celebrating the journey of growth and transformation together.

How to Navigate Challenges and Setbacks?

Life's journey is rarely a smooth sail; it's more like a series of waves, some gentle, others tumultuous. Similarly, when you begin to trust your intuition and follow its guidance, you may encounter obstacles that test your resolve and shake your confidence. These challenges can take many forms—from external circumstances such as financial setbacks or relationship struggles to internal barriers like self-doubt and fear of failure.

One of the first steps in overcoming challenges is to acknowledge their existence and accept that they are a natural part of the journey. Rather than viewing setbacks as roadblocks, see them as opportunities for growth and learning. Each obstacle you encounter is a chance to develop resilience, resourcefulness, and inner strength.

To navigate through challenges effectively, it's essential to cultivate a mindset of perseverance and adaptability. This means being open to change, embracing uncertainty, and learning from setbacks rather than allowing them to deter you from your path. Remember that the most significant growth often occurs during times of struggle, so don't shy away from challenges; face them head-on with courage and determination.

In addition to cultivating a resilient mindset, having a support system in place can also be instrumental in overcoming challenges. Surround yourself with people who believe in you, encourage you, and are willing to lend a helping hand when needed. Whether it's friends, family, mentors, or like-minded individuals on a similar journey, having a supportive community can provide the strength and motivation to persevere through tough times.

Another effective strategy for navigating challenges is to break them down into smaller, more manageable tasks. When faced with a daunting obstacle, it's easy to feel overwhelmed and paralyzed by the enormity of the challenge. By breaking it down into smaller steps and focusing on tackling one thing at a time, you can make progress gradually and build momentum toward overcoming the obstacle.

It's also essential to stay adaptable and flexible in your approach. What worked yesterday may not work today, and that's okay. Be willing to adjust your strategies, pivot when necessary, and explore alternative solutions to overcome obstacles. Remember, there's often more than one way to reach your destination; be open to exploring different paths and options along the way.

Navigating challenges and setbacks on your intuitive journey requires a combination of resilience, adaptability, and perseverance. By cultivating a mindset of growth and learning, seeking support when needed, breaking down obstacles into manageable tasks, and staying flexible in your approach, you can navigate through even the most turbulent waters and emerge stronger, wiser, and more empowered than ever before. So, embrace the challenges that come your way, for they are not obstacles but opportunities in disguise, guiding you toward greater self-discovery and fulfillment.

Prioritize Mental Health

In the journey of sharpening intuition and making things happen, mental health stands as the cornerstone of well-being. Amid the hustle and bustle of modern life, it's easy to overlook the importance of mental well-being, yet it is fundamental to our ability to connect with our intuition and navigate through life's twists and turns.

The modern world often places undue emphasis on physical health while neglecting the equally crucial aspect of mental well-being. However, the two are deeply interconnected, with mental health serving as the bedrock upon which physical health, emotional stability, and intuitive clarity rest. Just as we invest time and effort into maintaining our physical fitness, so too must we prioritize our mental fitness through practices that promote self-care, self-awareness, and emotional resilience.

One of the first steps in prioritizing mental health is to recognize and acknowledge its importance in our lives. Mental health encompasses not only the absence of mental illness but also the presence of positive mental states, such as happiness, fulfillment, and inner peace. By recognizing mental health as a priority, we can begin to cultivate habits and practices that nourish our minds and nurture our emotional well-being.

Central to prioritizing mental health is the practice of self-care, which involves taking deliberate actions to nurture and replenish ourselves on a physical, emotional, and spiritual level. This may include activities such as exercise, proper nutrition, adequate sleep, relaxation techniques, and engaging in hobbies or activities that bring joy and fulfillment. By making self-care a priority in our daily lives, we can better manage stress, reduce anxiety, and cultivate a greater sense of well-being.

Another essential aspect of prioritizing mental health is cultivating self-awareness, which involves developing an understanding of our thoughts, feelings, and behaviors. Through practices such as mindfulness meditation, journaling, or therapy, we can deepen our self-awareness and gain insight into the underlying causes of stress, anxiety, or other mental health challenges. By acknowledging and addressing these underlying issues, we can begin to cultivate greater emotional resilience and inner peace.

Furthermore, it's essential to cultivate healthy coping mechanisms for dealing with stress and adversity. Rather than turning to unhealthy habits such as substance abuse or avoidance, seek out positive coping strategies such as exercise, meditation, creative expression, or seeking support from friends, family, or mental health professionals. By developing healthy coping mechanisms, we can better manage life's challenges and navigate through difficult times with grace and resilience.

Finally, it's crucial to destigmatize mental health and encourage open dialogue about our struggles and challenges. Too often, individuals suffer in silence due to fear of judgment or shame surrounding mental illness. By fostering a culture of acceptance, understanding, and support, we can create a safe space for individuals to seek help and receive the support they need to thrive.

Prioritizing mental health is not only essential for our overall well-being but also foundational to our ability to connect with our intuition and make informed decisions in life. By cultivating habits and practices that promote self-care, self-awareness, and emotional resilience, we can lay the groundwork for intuitive success and live a more fulfilling and authentic life. That's why we have to commit to prioritizing our mental health and nurturing our minds with the same care and attention we devote to our physical health, for in doing so, we unlock the keys to greater happiness, fulfillment, and intuitive clarity.

Be Mindful and Meditate

In this chaotic modern life, where distractions abound and demands never cease, finding moments of stillness and clarity can feel like an elusive dream. Yet it is amid the calm of a quiet mind that intuition flourishes, guiding us toward our true purpose and potential. In this section, we explore the transformative power of meditation and mindfulness as essential tools for sharpening intuition and navigating life's journey with greater clarity and purpose.

Meditation and mindfulness are ancient practices that have stood the test of time, revered by sages, scholars, and seekers alike for their profound ability to quiet the mind and awaken inner wisdom. At their core, both practices invite us to cultivate a state of present-moment awareness, free from the distractions of the past and the worries of the future. By anchoring our attention to the here and now, we create space for intuition to speak and insights to arise.

One important element in the practice of meditation is the cultivation of inner stillness and focused attention. Through techniques such as breath awareness, body scan, or mantra repetition, we learn to quiet the chatter of the mind and enter a state of deep relaxation and receptivity. In this state of inner calm, we become more attuned to the subtle whispers of intuition, which often emerge when the mind is quiet and receptive.

Mindfulness, on the other hand, is about bringing awareness to our present-moment experience with openness, curiosity, and nonjudgment. Whether it's eating a meal, walking in nature, or engaging in everyday tasks, mindfulness invites us to fully immerse ourselves in the richness of each moment, awakening our senses and deepening our connection to the world around us. In doing so, we cultivate a heightened sense of clarity, insight, and intuition.

Integrating meditation and mindfulness into our daily lives need not be complicated or time-consuming. Even just a few minutes of practice each day can yield profound benefits for our mental, emotional, and spiritual well-being. Whether it's carving out time for a formal meditation session or infusing moments of mindfulness into our daily routines, consistency is key. Like tending to a garden, regular practice nurtures the seeds of intuition, allowing them to blossom and flourish over time.

Moreover, meditation and mindfulness offer a myriad of benefits beyond sharpening intuition. Research published in the *International Journal of Yoga* has shown that regular practice can reduce stress, anxiety, and depression, improve focus and concentration, enhance creativity and problem-solving skills, and cultivate a greater sense of overall well-being. By making meditation and mindfulness a regular part of our lives, we not only deepen our connection to intuition but also cultivate greater resilience, clarity, and presence in all areas of our lives.

To sum it up, meditation and mindfulness are powerful allies on the journey of intuitive discovery, offering a sanctuary of stillness amid the chaos of modern life. By cultivating a practice of presence and awareness, individuals create the conditions for intuition to thrive, which guides them toward greater clarity, purpose, and fulfillment.

Just Relax

Relaxation is not just about zoning out or numbing ourselves to the world; it's about intentionally creating space in our lives to unwind, de-stress, and rejuvenate. One powerful tool for relaxation is deep breathing exercises, which can be done anywhere, anytime, and require nothing more than a few moments of focused attention on the breath. By taking slow, deep breaths in through the nose, filling the lungs with air, and exhaling slowly through the mouth, we activate the body's relaxation response, calming the nervous system and promoting a sense of peace and well-being.

Another effective strategy for relaxation is progressive muscle relaxation, which involves systematically tensing and then releasing different muscle groups in the body. Starting with the toes and working our way up to the scalp, we tense each muscle group for a few seconds before releasing the tension and allowing the muscles to relax completely. This technique not only relieves physical tension and discomfort but also promotes a sense of deep relaxation and tranquility throughout the body and mind.

Engaging in leisure activities that bring us joy, pleasure, and a sense of fulfillment is another essential aspect of relaxation. Whether it's reading a book, gardening, painting, or playing a musical instrument, taking time to engage in activities that nourish our souls and rejuvenate our spirits is crucial for maintaining balance and well-being. By making time for leisure and relaxation, we can replenish our energy, reduce stress, and foster a greater sense of happiness and contentment in our lives.

Creating a calming environment that supports relaxation and well-being is also key. This may involve decluttering our living space, adding elements of nature such as plants or natural light, or creating a designated relaxation area where we can retreat and unwind. By consciously cultivating an environment that promotes relaxation and self-care, we can create the conditions for intuitive clarity to thrive, guiding us toward greater insight, creativity, and fulfillment.

Relaxation is a vital aspect of sharpening intuition and navigating life's challenges with clarity and purpose. By incorporating techniques such as deep breathing exercises, progressive muscle relaxation, and engaging in leisure activities into our daily routine, and creating a supportive environment that fosters relaxation and well-being, we can cultivate greater calm, clarity, and resilience in the face of life's demands. For all these reasons, we must prioritize relaxation as an essential aspect of our self-care routine, knowing that by nurturing our inner peace, we empower ourselves to live a life of greater joy, fulfillment, and intuitive clarity.

Seek Support for Mental Health

In the quest for self-improvement and intuitive clarity, one of the most profound acts of self-love and wisdom is recognizing when to seek help. Mental health is a cornerstone of well-being, and yet, societal stigma often shrouds it in silence and shame.

The journey of life is seldom traversed alone, and yet, many of us hesitate to reach out for help when we need it most. Whether due to pride, fear, or misconceptions about mental illness, seeking support for mental health can be a daunting prospect. However, it is precisely in those moments of vulnerability that our intuition speaks loudest and guides us toward the support and resources we need to heal and thrive.

One of the first steps in honoring our intuition in seeking support is recognizing the signs that indicate when help may be needed. These signs can vary widely and may include persistent feelings of sadness or anxiety, difficulty coping with stress, changes in sleep or appetite, social withdrawal, or difficulty functioning in daily life. By tuning into our intuition and paying attention to these warning signs, we can begin to acknowledge our need for support and take proactive steps toward healing.

It's essential to remember that seeking help is not a sign of weakness but rather a courageous act of self-awareness and self-care. Just as we wouldn't hesitate to seek medical attention for a physical ailment, so too should we prioritize our mental health and seek support when needed. Whether it's therapy, counseling, support groups, or medication, there are a myriad of resources available to support mental well-being, and it's important to explore what works best for us.

Moreover, seeking support for mental health is not just about alleviating symptoms; it's also about fostering a deeper sense of self-awareness, growth, and empowerment. Therapy, in particular, offers a safe and confidential space to explore our thoughts, feelings, and experiences, gain insight into underlying patterns and behaviors, and develop coping strategies for managing stress and adversity. Through the therapeutic process, we can cultivate greater resilience, self-compassion, and emotional well-being, ultimately leading to a more fulfilling and authentic life.

In addition to professional support, it's essential to cultivate a support network of friends, family, and loved ones who can offer understanding, encouragement, and empathy. Social support plays a crucial role in mental health and can provide a sense of belonging, validation, and connection during difficult times. By surrounding ourselves with people who uplift and support us, we create a foundation of strength and resilience from which to navigate life's challenges.

In conclusion, honoring our intuition in seeking support for mental health is a courageous and transformative step toward greater healing, growth, and self-discovery. When we recognize the signs that indicate when help may be needed, by overcoming stigma and misconceptions and reaching out for support when needed, we can cultivate greater resilience, self-awareness, and well-being. So, we should listen to the whispers of intuition, embrace the support and resources available to us, and journey toward greater healing, wholeness, and intuitive clarity.

Celebrate Progress and Growth

As we reach the culmination of our journey toward sharpening intuition and making things happen, it's essential to pause and reflect on the progress we've made, the challenges we've overcome, and the growth we've experienced along the way.

The path of self-improvement and intuitive clarity is not a linear one; it's a journey filled with twists, turns, and unexpected detours. Along the way, we encounter challenges that test our resolve, setbacks that shake our confidence, and moments of uncertainty that challenge our faith in ourselves and our intuition. And yet it is precisely in these moments of struggle that we find the seeds of growth and transformation.

One of the most powerful tools for nurturing intuition and fostering personal growth is the practice of self-reflection. By taking time to pause, look inward, and examine our thoughts, feelings, and experiences, we gain valuable insight into our inner world and the patterns that shape our lives. Through journaling or simply quiet contemplation, we can deepen our understanding of ourselves, our values, and our aspirations, paving the way for greater clarity, purpose, and direction.

Moreover, it's essential to approach self-reflection with an attitude of self-compassion and nonjudgment. Too often, we are our harshest critics, berating ourselves for perceived failures, shortcomings, or mistakes. However, true growth and transformation arise not from self-criticism but from self-compassion—the ability to acknowledge our humanity, embrace our imperfections, and treat ourselves with kindness and understanding. By cultivating self-compassion, we create a nurturing inner environment in which intuition can thrive, guiding us toward greater authenticity, fulfillment, and well-being.

In addition to self-reflection and self-compassion, it's essential to celebrate our progress and achievements along the journey. Each step we take, no matter how small, brings us closer to our goals and aspirations, and it's important to acknowledge and honor our efforts along the way. Whether it's completing a challenging task, overcoming a fear, or making a positive change in our lives, every accomplishment is a testament to our strength, resilience, and determination.

Furthermore, it's essential to recognize that growth is a lifelong journey, and there will always be new challenges to face, lessons to learn, and opportunities for growth and development. Rather than viewing setbacks as failures, see them as opportunities for growth and learning, and approach each challenge with curiosity, openness, and a willingness to learn. That way, you can continue to nurture intuition, deepen your self-awareness, and live a life of greater purpose, passion, and fulfillment.

By cultivating a practice of self-reflection, self-compassion, and celebration, we can nurture intuition, deepen our connection to ourselves and others, and live a life of greater clarity, authenticity, and fulfillment. Pause, reflect, and celebrate the journey you've traveled, knowing that the best is yet to come and the path ahead is filled with infinite possibilities for growth, learning, and intuitive clarity.

Conclusion

In this final chapter, "Get Your Sh** Together," we've delved into the inevitable challenges and setbacks that accompany the journey of honing our intuition. From unexpected obstacles to moments of doubt, we've acknowledged these hurdles as opportunities for growth and self-discovery. Here, we've outlined strategies for navigating these challenges with resilience and grace, emphasizing the importance of prioritizing mental health, mindfulness, seeking support, relaxation, and celebrating progress and growth.

Life's journey is fraught with challenges, but by adopting a mindset of perseverance and adaptability, we can overcome obstacles and emerge stronger. Cultivating resilience, seeking support, and breaking down challenges into manageable tasks are crucial steps in navigating through turbulent times. Additionally, prioritizing mental health through self-care, self-awareness, and healthy coping mechanisms is fundamental to nurturing our intuition.

Mindfulness and meditation serve as powerful tools for quieting the mind and fostering a deeper connection with our intuition. By practicing present-moment awareness, we create space for intuition to thrive and guide us toward greater clarity and purpose.

Relaxation plays a vital role in sharpening intuition, allowing us to unwind and replenish our energy amid life's demands. Techniques such as deep breathing exercises, progressive muscle relaxation, and engaging in leisure activities promote a sense of calm and well-being, nurturing our inner peace and clarity.

Seeking support for mental health is an act of courage and self-love, essential for healing and growth. Whether through therapy, counseling, or social support, reaching out for help fosters greater resilience and emotional well-being.

Finally, celebrating progress and growth along the journey reminds us of our strength, resilience, and determination. By practicing self-reflection, self-compassion, and gratitude, we honor our efforts and embrace the infinite possibilities for growth and intuitive clarity that lie ahead.

In conclusion, the journey of sharpening intuition is not without its challenges, but by embracing resilience, prioritizing mental health, practicing mindfulness, seeking support, and celebrating progress, we can navigate through life's twists and turns with grace and purpose. Trust in your intuition, embrace the journey, and know that the path ahead is filled with boundless opportunities for growth, learning, and fulfillment.

Conclusion

As we draw the curtains on this journey toward sharpening your intuition, let's take a moment to bask in the glow of your growth and newfound wisdom. The path you've walked has been illuminated by the light of your intuition, guiding you through the labyrinth of self-discovery and transformation.

Throughout this book, we've peeled back the layers of intuition, revealing its intricate workings and empowering you with practical tools to harness its power. From meditation practices to dissecting dreams, from understanding subconscious processes to refining your intuitive skills, you've embarked on a journey of self-discovery and growth.

But beyond the techniques and exercises lies a deeper truth: intuition is more than just a skill—it's a sacred connection to the universe, a compass that points toward your true north. It's the whispers of your soul, the echoes of your deepest desires, urging you to step boldly into the unknown and embrace the adventure that lies ahead.

And while our journey together may be coming to an end, your journey toward self-mastery is just beginning. Like a seed planted in fertile soil, your intuition will continue to blossom and flourish with nurturing and care. So tend to it with love, cultivate it with mindfulness, and watch as it blooms into a radiant beacon of guidance and wisdom.

As you navigate the twists and turns of life's great adventure, remember to trust in the wisdom of your intuition. It's your inner compass, your faithful guide, leading you toward the paths that resonate with your soul's purpose. Embrace its whispers, for they carry the secrets of the universe and the keys to your deepest fulfillment.

And should you ever find yourself at a crossroads, uncertain of which path to take, pause for a moment, and listen to the gentle whispers of your intuition. For within its sacred chambers lies the answer you seek, waiting patiently to be discovered.

So, my dear friend, as we bid adieu to this chapter of our journey, let us carry forth the lessons learned and the wisdom gained. Continue to walk with courage, dance with joy, and make sh** happen in every corner of your life.

And if your intuition is nudging you to explore further, trust that it's guiding you toward other titles in this series. So, heed its call, for within the pages of these books, you may find further insights and inspiration to fuel your journey of self-discovery and growth.

For in the end, it is not the destination that matters, but the journey itself—the journey of self-discovery, growth, and transformation. And with your intuition as your faithful guide, there is no doubt that your path will be filled with wonder, joy, and endless possibilities.

Keep shining brightly, keep trusting in your intuition, and keep making sh** happen.

With boundless gratitude and admiration,

Deborah LeBlanc

Bibliography

Black, David S., Gillian A. O'Reilly, Richard Olmstead, Elizabeth C. Breen, and Michael R. Irwin. "Mindfulness Meditation and Improvement in Sleep Quality and Daytime Impairment among Older Adults With Sleep Disturbances: A Randomized Clinical Trial." *JAMA Internal Medicine* 175, no. 4 (2015):494–501. https://doi.org/10.1001/jamainternmed.2014.8081.

Galante, Julieta, Ignacio Galante, Marie-Jet Bekkers, and John Gallacher. "Effect of Kindness-Based Meditation on Health and Well-Being: A Systematic Review and Meta-Analysis." *Journal of Consulting and Clinical Psychology* 82 (2014):1101–1114. https://doi.org/10.1037/a0037249.

Lieberman, Matthew D. "Intuition: A Social Cognitive Neuroscience Approach." *Psychological Bulletin* 126, no. 1 (2000): 109–137. https://doi.org/10.1037/0033-2909.126.1.109.

Pacini, Rosemary, and Seymour Epstein. "The Relation of Rational and Experiential Information Processing Styles to Personality, Basic Beliefs, and the Ratio-Bias Phenomenon." *Journal of Personality and Social Psychology* 76, no. 6 (1999): 972–987. https://doi.org/10.1037/0022-3514.76.6.972.

Pretz, Jean E., and Kathryn Sentman Totz. "Measuring Individual Differences in Affective, Heuristic, and Holistic Intuition." *Personality and Individual Differences, 43 no.* 5 (2007): 1247–1257. https://doi.org/10.1016/j.paid.2007.03.015.

Weir, Kirsten. "Nurtured by Nature." *Monitor on Psychology* 51, no. 3 (2020). https://www.apa.org/monitor/2020/04/nurtured-nature.

Woodyard, Catherine. "Exploring the Therapeutic Effects of Yoga and Its Ability to Increase Quality of Life." *International Journal of Yoga* 4, no. 2 (2011): 49–54. https://doi.org/10.4103%2F0973-6131.85485.

Yeh Chin-Wen, Shih-Han Hung, and Chun-Yen Chang. "The Influence of Natural Environments on Creativity." *Frontiers in Psychiatry* 13 (July 27, 2022): 895213. https://doi.org/10.3389/fpsyt.2022.895213.

www.ingramcontent.com/pod-product-compliance
Lightning Source LLC
Chambersburg PA
CBHW070112080526
44586CB00013B/1269